We Fear N

A decade of following Millwall

Colin Johnson

A TERRACE BANTER PUBLICATION

*To Gavin, Jason, Lena and George for their words of encouragement
and advice, and to all Millwall fans who make the effort
to continually follow their team, through thick and thin,
and despite all the bullshit and hassle. Let 'em come!*

We Fear No Foe - A Decade Of Following Millwall (Pbk)

© Colin Johnson, 1999

ISBN 0 9535920 2 2

Published by Terrace Banter, Scotland
Printed by Victoria Press, England

A Terrace Banter publication from
S.T. Publishing
P.O. Box 12, Lockerbie, Dumfriesshire. DG11 3BW. Scotland.
stpbooks@aol.com

SOCCER THUGS PLOTTED RIOT

SCUM!

FA roar warning to Lions

15-MINUTE MAYHEM ROCKS OUR HOPES OF A RETURN TO EUROPE

RIOT ACT

With broken posts, a ripped-up pitch and attacks on directors and police

INTRODUCTION

The first match I recall watching on television was during the 1978 World Cup in Argentina. England had failed to qualify for this tournament and the sole representatives from Great Britain were Scotland. As always, the national press expected the English to get behind the Scots and cheer them on to victory. My father is a passionate Scot, so much so that he left his beloved homeland at the age of 15, and after serving in the Royal Navy, settled down in South East England, well away from the hills and glens so loved by all Scots.

Encouraged by the media and my father, I cheered Ally McLeod's tartan army in their games against Iran and Peru. The results did not quite go their way, and so in the final game they had to beat Holland by three clear goals to qualify for the second phase. At the time this seemed an impossible task, but Scotland performed bravely and eventually won the game 3-2. Unfortunately for them, it was not enough to qualify, and so the Scots returned home early as usual.

One positive outcome of Scotland's dismal performance though was that my love of football escalated after this tournament, but coming from Surrey it was not clear who I should support. My father was not a true football fan although he claimed to support Glasgow Rangers. In reality this was only because he had been raised as a Protestant in Glasgow and had enjoyed fighting the Tims every New Year in his younger days. He encouraged me to support Rangers, but most of all he insisted I hate Celtic. To this day, I don't really care about Rangers, but I do hate Celtic and everything they stand for.

Up until the age of about 12, I played football continuously, read *Shoot and Match* every week, and religiously watched *On The Ball*, *Football Focus*, *Match Of The Day* and *The Big Match*. Liverpool and Arsenal were the successful teams in those days and most of the boys at school supported one of them, but for me life was never quite that simple.

My Mum and Dad were divorced, and so when my Dad secured a job in New Cross and moved to Catford, I spent every second weekend in South East London. Usually my dad would pick me up from Waterloo and drive down the Old Kent Road, through

New Cross, and on to Catford, and as we made the journey, he'd regularly mention that Millwall played at The Den, somewhere in the back streets just off the Old Kent Road. I always found this a little curious as no floodlights were visible from my vantage point, and even on match days you very rarely saw a football crowd in the area.

Most Saturday and Sunday lunchtimes would be spent in the pubs of New Cross. I was a fairly quiet boy and would only really join in with the conversations if they were about football. One of the drinking crowd was a Ugandan by the name of Moses. We would always discuss football, and as I was now becoming obsessed with visiting The Den, I would badger him about taking me down there. Moses was as black as the ace of spades and was never really keen on going to The Den, but as a compromise he took me to The Valley to watch Charlton play Newcastle United. This was when the Geordies were building a really good team, with the likes of Keegan, Beardsley, McDermott and Waddle playing. They won the game convincingly and eventually gained promotion that season. I recall walking to the ground and noticing that Newcastle supporters were everywhere. So much so in fact that I refused to go in the Charlton end, and we watched the game with the Geordies.

The Valley was a huge stadium, but the home support was completely inadequate and I felt really embarrassed for the Charlton fans. Even at that tender age I became aware of the importance of protecting your home ground from away fans. The Valley has now been refurbished, but the home support hasn't really changed. It would appear that Charlton fans have very little passion and are unable to offer the partisan support that a team should expect from their own supporters. No wonder Millwall laugh at the Charlton fans.

Luckily, this trip did not serve its purpose and I failed to become an anorak. I continued to hound Moses about taking me to The Den, but in November, 1985, Millwall played Leeds at home. This match was marred by serious disturbances, and Moses himself was racially abused by Leeds fans in New Cross before the game.

After the Leeds game, Millwall were heavily fined by the FA and ordered to make games at The Den all ticket. This made it even more difficult for supporters to attend the games and attendances dropped quite considerably. These events naturally enough encouraged Moses to keep me away from The Den, but in all truth they just enhanced my determination to go.

In January, 1986, Millwall were drawn at home to Wimbledon in the Third Round of the FA Cup. The Dons were an up and coming team at the time, and I was determined to make my first visit to The Den. Quite understandably, Moses refused to come with me, but kindly offered to get me two tickets for the game anyway.

I managed to talk my mate Terry, an Arsenal fan, into taking the spare ticket, and on the day of the match, we made our way through the maze of back streets and stumbled upon The Den. You would never have known that you were in the vicinity of one of the most notorious football grounds in the UK until you turned the corner into Cold Blow Lane. We had arrived early and the area was still quiet. Most supporters were still in the pubs so we used this opportunity to have a good look around. It was a drab and depressing place with graffiti and barbed wire everywhere. Once inside the ground, my initial impression did not change. It looked like a ground that you would find in East Berlin rather than South East London. There was an eerie feeling in the air, something I have not experienced at any other ground in England.

The ground did not really fill up until kick-off. However, at about two o'clock, 500 or so Wimbledon fans entered the ground under heavy police escort. They were singing and shouting and appeared to be having a more enjoyable time than the few Millwall fans inside the ground at the time. We went over to the North terrace, otherwise known as the Halfway, to be closer to the away fans, and when the game kicked off, the home supporters came to life. Whilst the away fans were silent, the noise generated by the 5,000 Millwall supporters was deafening. The continuous chant of "Milllllwallll!" echoed all around the ground. I was transfixed to my spot on the Halfway, surrounded by large men in their thirties and forties who were getting behind their team with a passion the likes of which I had never seen before. Certainly not at the few Aldershot games I had been to with my school mates anyway. Stood around me were the men who had battled their way around the lower leagues for years, earning themselves a fearful reputation throughout the country.

Millwall beat Wimbledon 3-1 and as far as I know there were no violent incidents at this game. I did not attend another game for 18 months, but despite this I now classed myself as a Millwall fan and found myself defending the honour of Millwall supporters when they made headlines for all the wrong reasons at Southampton and Portsmouth later that season.

Early in the 1987-88 season, Millwall were drawn away to West Ham in the SIMOD Cup. The Irons and Millwall were bitter rivals, but the two sides had not played each other since the late Seventies. That game had been marred by serious violence and ever since then the fans of both sides had been involved in a sort of cold war. The fans would clash at any opportunity at locations throughout the country, and the disturbances to date had left two people dead (one from each side) and many more seriously hurt. Both sides claimed to be victorious on many occasions, but the SIMOD Cup match was the perfect opportunity to settle all the old scores.

The game itself was not an attractive prospect for most normal fans as the SIMOD Cup was generally considered two bob. However, for the boys from both teams, it was too good an opportunity to miss. In the weeks building up to the game, battles were planned at various locations throughout South East and East London. Men who had not been to football for years were tempted out of retirement to attend this game with the sole intention of inflicting physical damage on their opponents. While all this was going on, the Metropolitan Police were planning the largest ever police operation for a match in London, not counting Cup finals or internationals held at Wembley. All police leave was suspended and extra officers were even drafted in from Kent.

Back in Surrey, I was oblivious to all that was going on, and had arranged to attend this match with three friends who I had managed to persuade to come along with me. We were all aware that there might be some trouble at the game, but we had all seen it go off at some of the Aldershot games we had attended, and the prospect of trouble just made the game all the more attractive to us wide eyed innocents.

And so it was that four boys travelled into London for a game that was to have a profound effect on all our lives. The events that unfolded before our eyes had a huge impact on all of us. One lad was so scared that he only ever attended Aldershot games afterwards. The other two were so enthralled at what they witnessed that they regularly started to go to football in an effort to recapture the buzz that they experienced that night. One of the boys was an Arsenal fan and he started going to Arsenal every week where he quickly became part of the casual scene at Highbury. The other lad went anywhere he could to capture the buzz and regularly came along to The Den with me. For the first couple of years we made a point of looking out for the trouble, but in the early Nineties we made a concerted effort to avoid it. In a bid to find a new release from the

7

misery of every day life, my friend took to drugs and died a few years later.

As for me, I have now been following Millwall, home and away for 12 years. I have had many laughs, enjoyed a good drink, and met many characters, some rather unsavoury, but many as genuine as they come. I have been involved in some notorious incidents and witnessed many more. I have been hurt on a few occasions and experienced extreme fear. I have travelled extensively, both in England following Millwall, and in Europe following England. I have gained a keen interest in the casual scene at football and always dress in a casual way when I attend games.

For all that, I am not a top boy, a face, or even an active hooligan. I am a casually dressed football fan who enjoys a good drink and a laugh with his mates on a Saturday afternoon. I am just like thousands of other young men throughout the country. I always try to avoid the violence at football, but sometimes this just isn't possible.

Not all hooligans are casuals, and not all casuals are hooligans. I don't usually travel to a game mob handed, I prefer to travel with just one or two close friends. We try to keep ourselves to ourselves and our intention is to have a good drink in another town and watch the football, without any trouble. However, as a result of the way we dress, our age, and the reputation of our team, violence can come looking for you no matter how hard you try to avoid it. On days like this, we make an effort to stick with the travelling support. As a lot of these supporters are also young casual lads, a mob is usually formed and violence sometimes erupts. Although this is not what I am looking for, it is usually safer to attend these games in a mob. If trouble does occur, the police are usually on top of the situation immediately, and although hundreds of people may be present, only a handful get actively involved in any violence. There is no requirement to be a hard man at Millwall, although you must have a bit of bottle and loyalty to your mates and fellow supporters.

The tabloid press have stereotyped all Millwall supporters for a number of years now, certainly longer than I have been going, and appear to be leading a crusade to get the club shut down. They have done such a good job that the words "Millwall" and "hooligan" appear to be entwined, and people who have never been to a match in their life consider all Millwall fans to be a bunch of moronic hooligans. I will not deny that there is a hooligan element amongst the Millwall support, but the football club and the local police have done all they can to eradicate the problem. Every club in the country has a hooligan problem, and Millwall are by no means an exception. The truth though is that Millwall do not have the largest or even the most active hooligans in the country.

The purpose of this book is to show what it is really like to follow Millwall. I will explain what really went on at some of the games that have now become infamous for the violence that surrounded them. I will also look at how these events were reported in the press and seek to question why they always seem to be reported in the same hysterical manner. Hopefully, the book will appeal to Millwall supporters and also to certain supporters of other clubs. By this, I mean the real supporters - people who attended the games before the sport became fashionable with the middle classes. The people who stood on the terraces in the freezing cold, people who coped with draconian policing, and people who had to put up with nonsense from British Rail and the like.

The new wave of football fans who appeared on the scene after the 1990 World Cup will probably not be interested in what I have to say and may even find some of the comments in this book offensive. They will not be able to relate to what happens, simply because their idea of watching football is to snuggle up on the sofa with the wife and watch the live Sky game in the warmth of their own home. These people may consider themselves to be football fans, but in my opinion you are not a true supporter of your team unless you regularly attend games.

It is the real fans who create the atmosphere that makes the game so exciting. A football crowd should not be like a theatre or cinema audience, it should be an integral part of the event. They should not be afraid to voice their anger or to intimidate the opposition and their fans.

There seems to be a conspiracy in place to keep these genuine fans away from football and replace them with quiet, appreciative new fans who are happy to spend extortionate amounts of money on club merchandise. These people may be quite content in the present climate, but if the bubble bursts it will be the real fans the clubs will be forced to turn to, and this should never be forgotten by anyone involved in the game.

CHAPTER 1

Throughout the world, in all forms of life, rivalries exist. Britain is certainly no different in this respect, and football fans in particular thrive on competition. In England for example, there is an intense rivalry between Northerners and Southerners. In addition, people from different areas of the north, such as Lancashire and Yorkshire, tend to dislike each other just as much as, say, in Hampshire, Portsmouth and Southampton fans hate each other with venom (and although Portsmouth have a large hooligan following who travel throughout the country, their primary aim seems to be to fight fans from Southampton at any given opportunity).

In the South East, the rivalries are not so intense. Counties such as Surrey and Kent are not real football hotbeds, and most people from these areas tend to follow one of the London teams anyway. Londoners tend to dislike anyone from outside London. Pure and simple. They consider Northerners to be divs, and people from the West or the East to be country bumpkins. People from these areas are generally treated with contempt and little respect, and this may explain why Londoners are so reviled by most other football fans in England. And although most Londoners dislike outsiders, they are also not too keen on people from other parts of the city either. In fact, there has been a healthy rivalry between north and south London ever since London developed around the Thames into the prosperous capital city it is today.

Millwall Football Club, the Lions, was formed on the Isle Of Dogs in East London over 100 years ago. Shortly after their formation, they moved south of the river to New Cross and played their home games at The Den in Cold Blow Lane. Their fan base primarily comes from this small part of South East London, and it is fair to say that areas such as Bermondsey, Rotherhithe, New Cross, Walworth, Camberwell, Peckham, and Deptford, are recognised as being Millwall areas. This part of London is very run down and is dominated by large housing estates. Unemployment and racial tension is rife in areas such as this. South East London has a reputation for producing notorious gangsters and fearless boxers, and it is said that there are more dead bodies in the Thames by Bermondsey than in any other stretch of the river. The police have little respect in the community, and if someone has a problem that needs sorting out, the police seldom get involved. Disputes are often settled violently and people who grass to the authorities pay the price or leave the area.

It comes as no surprise to me that when thousands of young men from this area congregate in a football stadium to watch their local team play that tempers often flare. And if a mob of other young men from similar estates in other parts of the country are also present, the prospects of serious disorder are obvious to anyone with half a brain. Football, whether the authorities like it or not, provides the perfect arena.

A large police presence is just as likely to increase the chances of violence rather than decrease it, as many people consider the police fair game for attack. In fact, it is probably true to say that some people turn up with the sole intention of kicking it off with the police, and small incidents can escalate into a full scale riot very easily.

The young men from South East London tend to especially dislike their counterparts from the East End. This is nothing new, and back in the Fifties and Sixties rival gangsters from both areas were involved in many battles. West Ham United play in the heart of the East End and are considered by many Millwall fans to be our most hated rivals. When the two teams play each other, it provides the perfect opportunity for gangs from East and South East London to confront each other.

The two clubs have enjoyed rather different fortunes on the pitch in recent years, and prior to 1987 had not played each other for over ten years. Then, in 1987, the two teams were drawn to play each other at Upton Park in a meaningless SIMOD Cup match. For the casual young men from the estates however, it was far from meaningless.

The tube pulled into the Embankment tube station and the four of us got on. The tube was fairly busy, mainly with commuters, but also what looked like a few young men on their way to Upton Park. We settled down for the long journey through the East End and chatted quite happily amongst ourselves.

A few more boys got on at various stations along the way and then the tube pulled into Whitechapel. I had thought a few Millwall might get on here as this station connects with the East London line for Rotherhithe and Surrey Docks. As the tube pulled in, the platform was full of blokes in their late twenties. Unlike most football crowds, this mob was deadly quiet and looked more than a little menacing. Not one fan had any identifying colours, and as they boarded the tube the silence was largely maintained. My friends and I had stopped chatting and were trying to listen to what the blokes next to us were saying. I was sure they were Millwall, but there was a possibility that they might have been West Ham. I was mightily relieved when I overheard the blokes chatting about the Aston Villa match from the previous weekend.

The tube eventually pulled into Mile End station. Even I was aware that this was West Ham territory and that the ICF often used The Horn And Plenty pub outside the station, and I feared an ambush. When the tube doors opened, the train emptied. We remained on the tube as Millwall firmed up on the platform, and then as we started to make our way to the exit, there was a deafening roar. I could not see exactly what was happening, but it was pretty obvious that there was some West Ham in the area. The mayhem continued for a couple of minutes. Police were now in the station in numbers and were forcing Millwall back onto the tube, much to the horror of the commuters returning home.

The tube set off on its journey and the atmosphere on the train had changed. The blokes involved in the disturbance were talking quickly and seemed to be buzzing as if they were on some sort of a drug. There was a small police presence on the tube now, but this was not enough to reassure the terrified commuters. Me, I was excited at the prospect of what lay ahead. I had been to Upton Park and was well aware that they normally had a few boys milling around the Queens market. With the numbers on our tube, I was quite sure we would easily see them off.

As we alighted at Upton Park, the drawn out chant of "Millllllwalllll!" echoed around the station. We walked up the stairs and out into Green Street. I had never seen so many police in my life. There were riot vans, dogs, horses, and even a helicopter in the sky above. The police would not let Millwall keep still and forced us to walk briskly down to the ground. In every side street on the way down to the ground mobs of West Ham boys were trying desperately to get at us. At the same time, the police were belting any Millwall that tried to break out of the escort. To be fair, the police did a fantastic job keeping the two sets of fans mostly apart. Had they been able to get at each other, there would certainly have been many serious casualties.

The escort turned left by the school and we queued up to pay at the turnstiles. The police had erected walk through metal detectors, the kind you see at the airports, and this generated a little panic amongst some of the Millwall. They darted off to some bushes and discarded a number of weapons. It later emerged that knives, axes, CS gas sprays, and various other weapons were found here by the police.

The metal detectors had delayed our entry into the ground and when the game kicked off with all of us still outside, an attempt was made to surge through the detectors and steam the gates. The police quickly ended this by charging into us on their horses and lashing out with their batons.

Eventually, I got into the ground and walked into the stadium. Millwall were penned into the corner of the South Bank, by the main stand. The other two sections of the South Bank were segregated. Half the Chicken Run was closed, and unsurprisingly, the family stand was virtually empty.

To our left, in the corner of the main stand, was the main bulk of West Ham. This part of the stand was full of their boys and what a good mob it was. Between the two sets of fans was a huge number of police clad in full riot gear.

As the game was played, the fans chose to front each other rather than watch the game. The Lions chanted, "You'll get the same as Luton!" and "We are evil!", whilst the West Ham continually chanted "ICF!". Coins and other missiles were launched between the two sets of fans throughout the game.

Suddenly, a large roar came from the North Bank. West Ham had scored. The ICF had not noticed as they were too busy keeping an eye on us. In turn, we had not seen the goal because of the huge amount of police in front of our end. The belated realisation that we were a goal down though was the spark for Millwall to try to launch a full scale pitch invasion. As the police battled with Millwall to prevent us gaining access to the playing area, they also had to contend with the ICF who were equally determined to join us on the pitch.

The police prevented the pitch invasion and the game continued in the same heavy atmosphere. Soon afterwards, West Ham were awarded a corner in front of the away support. Not one West Ham player wanted to come over to us to take the kick. You could see the players arguing with each other. Paul Ince was playing that night, but not even the self styled guvnor was keen to get too near to the Millwall supporters. Eventually, Mark Ward raced to the corner flag, placed the ball down and took the quickest corner kick you will ever see at a game.

As the game continued, rumours started flying around that Millwall had scored. After about 30 seconds, the away end started jumping for joy. The police line in front of the away end was five thick. The view from that end was poor at the best of times because the terrace was so shallow, but with so many police there, it was impossible to watch the game. If you have ever seen a video of this game, you will see Millwall score but you will not hear a cheer for a while afterwards.

Miraculously, Millwall scored again and the same delayed reaction erupted among the away fans. The West Ham fans were none too happy and made to leave the ground, but as they exited the main stand, they were charged back into the ground by the police.

Millwall won the game 2-1 and although the Millwall fans were happy with the result, they seemed to have other more important things on their minds. We were kept in the ground for a while and eventually let out under heavy escort. We made our way to the tube station in similar fashion to our earlier walk, with both groups of fans fighting with the police in an attempt to get at each other. The police put us on the tube and we left Upton Park. There were many police on our tube and also police at every station on the way to Whitechapel.

I am not a fan of the police, but I have to say they did an incredible job that night. There must have been three or four thousand men trying to fight each other, and by and large the police managed to keep them apart. I understand there were other major incidents at London Bridge and Liverpool Street that day, but I will not comment on what happened there as I was not present, but I dare say the police were on top.

The four of us returned home to Surrey that night amazed at what we had witnessed. I was sure it would be all over the newspapers the following day and was looking forward to telling my mates all about it, but when the papers came out there was hardly anything in them about the fighting. I am sure all my mates thought I was exaggerating, but I was on such a high that I just kept talking about it. Luckily, a few days later, there was a special report in the *Daily Mail* about the police operation, and thankfully, this backed up my stories.

I had experienced considerable fear that night and yet the adrenalin rush was incredible and lasted for days. I felt like a drug addict who had to get his next fix. Millwall were at home to Manchester City on the Saturday and I could not wait to go.

I attended the game, and although the atmosphere was nothing like the West Ham game, it was still fantastic. After the game, as I made my way back to New Cross station, I saw the Man City fans being escorted to the station. They looked a mean bunch and I later learned that they had been involved in another large scale fight with Millwall at London Bridge. I was rapidly learning that incidents such as this are a lot more common place than the media would have us believe. Unless there is trouble at the match itself, the violence tends not to get reported.

My next game was Blackburn away, a week later. I travelled up on the train to Preston and thought I would have a look around Preston before continuing my journey to Blackburn. A few other Millwall walked out of the station with me. The pub near the station was full of Preston boys, and I was not too happy about having to walk past them. I had witnessed Preston taking the Aldershot end earlier that year and was well aware that they had quite a few boys. Luckily, the police pulled us up and persuaded us to get over to Blackburn.

I made my way to the ground on my own. It was about two o'clock and there was hardly anyone around. This was before the Jack Walker days, the ground was run down and crowds were low. I was chatting to a policeman and asked him if there was anywhere I could get some food near the ground. I thought he might have misunderstood my Southern accent, as he advised me that I could get some pot in a local pub. When I told him that I didn't take drugs, he burst out laughing and told all his mates about the stupid Cockney called me.

I quickly moved on, and as I headed back to the ground I heard the reassuring chant of "Millllllwalllll!" echoing around the cobbled streets. About 300-400 fans were being escorted from the station. They were all men in their late twenties with no colours on, but it was not a mob in the normal sense. This was just the type of people who went to Millwall. They were in good spirits and did not appear to be looking for trouble. The turnstiles at Ewood Park were very narrow and one of the Millwall fans was so fat he actually got stuck. His mates had to push him through much to his embarrassment.

The Millwall supporters really got behind the team and I thoroughly enjoyed myself. After the game, we were all escorted back to the station. I enjoyed seeing the expressions on the faces of the local householders as the famous Millwall supporters were being marched through their town. The journey home was even more interesting as I got chatting to a few fans and heard some great stories about previous awaydays. This was definitely the way I wanted to spend my Saturdays in the future.

The following week I went to the Ipswich game at Portman Road. This trip sticks in my mind because at the final whistle the home fans were kept in whilst the police escorted Millwall to the station. Usually, it's the away fans who get kept in after a game. In fact, this is the only time I have ever seen this happen and could not imagine the Millwall fans putting up with such a gesture at The Den.

The draw for the Third Round of the FA Cup had been made, and much to my delight, Millwall had been drawn away at Arsenal. I managed to obtain a ticket for a seat in the visitors part of the West Stand, and on the day of the match I made my way to the Rose pub opposite New Cross Gate station where I had arranged to meet a bloke called Paul who I'd first met on the train going to Ipswich a few weeks earlier. Paul was a few years older than me, was game for a row, and for some strange reason loved the taste of cat food.

The atmosphere in the pub was wonderful. It was a glorious sunny winter's day and everyone was drinking and discussing the game. Millwall actually had a fairly good team and a few of us were anticipating a Cup shock. Meanwhile, in the build up to the game, the press had been anticipating trouble. The *Daily Mirror* had gone so far as to claim that we were planning to steal the clock from the Clock End. The Millwall fans found this hilarious, but the talk of trouble at the game only heightened our excitement.

We made our way to Charing Cross and caught a tube to take us to Highbury that was already full of chanting, drunk Millwall supporters. Japanese tourists stared in amazement, but continued to take photographs of us nonetheless. When we got to Highbury, we made our way into the ground. As we did so, a few Millwall fans, out to make a name for themselves, turned over a hot dog stall and stole the vendor's takings. I have never been impressed by petty crimes like this. If these boys really wanted trouble, there were plenty of Arsenal fans only too willing to oblige. If they were real hard men, they would be looking for Gooners instead of bullying an innocent man just trying to earn a living.

I took up my seat in the stand and noticed the bloke next to me was talking into a walkie-talkie. It was just my luck that I was seated next to a plain clothed copper. Suddenly, a large fight started in the North Bank. From where I was sat, I could not clearly see exactly what was happening, but there was obviously a mob of Millwall trying to take the North Bank. They were not having it all their own way though as a large number of Gooners raced across the terrace to help their mates.

As the police battled to quell the disorder in the North Bank, Millwall charged the Arsenal fans in their section of the Clock End. Once again, the Arsenal fans were only too happy to join in. Meanwhile, other Millwall supporters attacked the police at the front of the Clock End in an attempt to invade the pitch. All in all, there were three separate serious disturbances going on and the game had not even started.

The game kicked off slightly later than planned and sporadic outbursts of violence, mainly aimed at the police, continued throughout the match. Despite vociferous support from the Millwall supporters, the players failed to rise to the occasion and Arsenal won 2-0 to send us out of the Cup.

After the game, Millwall were escorted to Highbury & Islington tube station, but at the junction of the Holloway Road, Millwall burst through the police escort and charged up the Holloway Road. Arsenal did not appear to have a mob waiting up there so this seemed pretty pointless. There were small groups of Arsenal fans in the area and they were viciously attacked by large numbers of Millwall. I found the general disorder that surrounded this game to be great fun, but incidents such as this were out of order. If you are in a firm and are looking for trouble, you should never attack innocent supporters just to satisfy your desires. Every team has a mob and you should search for like minded people. There is nothing big about 20 or 30 blokes attacking one or two people just because they happen to support another team. Unfortunately, this still happens at Millwall. It happens elsewhere too, and I have been attacked in similar circumstances at Birmingham, Portsmouth and Sunderland. People who carry out attacks like this should be treated with contempt. They may think they are big hard men, but to me they are nobodies.

Luckily, the police came to the rescue of the Arsenal victims. Unfortunately, for the majority of the Millwall fans in the vicinity, the police do not tend to ask questions in situations like this. Batons were pulled and used on any Millwall fan within striking distance. We were chased down the spiral staircase inside the tube station while attempting to protect our heads from the blows. Really, the police were no better than the Millwall cowards who battered the Arsenal fans in the area. They attacked many innocent people that day, and by the looks on their faces, enjoyed doing it too.

The following day, the press went to town on the Millwall supporters. In addition to the incidents I witnessed, Millwall supporters had attacked two pubs outside the ground. The violence was bad by any standards and Millwall fans must hold their hands up, but Arsenal fans were only too happy to join in and it does take two to have a fight. There were no hysterical cries for Arsenal to be kicked out of the Cup though. In one paper, in bold letters was the headline SCUM, and underneath was a picture of Martin Hayes celebrating his goal. To be fair, I wouldn't blame poor old Martin for any of the trouble, and as for him being labelled scum . . . well, I don't know what the world's coming to.

With the Lions now out of the FA Cup, we were left to concentrate on the league and life in the old Division Two. As I mentioned earlier, we had a reasonable team at the time. Terry Hurlock and Les Briley were the backbone of a highly industrious outfit, with Hollywood superstar, Kevin O'Callaghan, playing on the wing, and Sherringham and Cascarino becoming quite a handful up front.

Although we did not hammer anyone and always seemed to make each game look more difficult than it actually was, we continued to grind out results and slowly climbed up the table. By the end of March, we were in shouting distance of an automatic promotion place. Suddenly, the fans realised that this could be the year when Millwall finally gained promotion.

On Easter Monday, Millwall were due to play away at Leeds United. Leeds were also chasing promotion and with the 1985 clashes between the fans still fresh in the memory, a good trip lay ahead. That was until the game was moved to the following Wednesday night without so much as a hint of an explanation. Millwall refused to lay on transport to the game for their own fans and British Rail announced that any Millwall supporters planning on making the trip would not be able to get home afterwards. It seemed that there was a conspiracy to prevent Millwall supporters attending this game, but of course this just made the Millwall fans even more determined to make the trip north.

I took the day off work and set off for Leeds at lunchtime. Although it was true that there was no direct trains from Leeds to

London after the game, I was certain that there would be a good mob of Millwall going up. And if that was the case, there was no way the police were going to leave us in Leeds after the game and I was sure they would force us onto a local train to Doncaster where we would be able to catch an overnight sleeper from Scotland or the North East.

On arrival at Kings Cross, I was pleased to see 60 or 70 Millwall milling around on the concourse. I recognised these faces from previous games and it is fair to say that these lads would probably be classed as the main firm. They were all casually dressed and certainly looked like they knew the score.

Prior to departure, I found a seat on the train and just as it was about to leave, the Millwall mob joined my carriage. Although they did not know me personally, it was obvious I was Millwall. I was on my own and one of them warned me that it would be dodgy in Leeds if I remained that way. He told me that they would be getting off in Wakefield for a drink, before catching a local bus into Leeds, and he advised me to stick with them which I was only too pleased to do.

The police had ordered the buffet not to serve alcohol. This was common practice at the time and came as no surprise to anyone. Some of the boys had managed to smuggle some vodka on to the train, but drink wasn't really the drug of choice what with most of them openly snorting lines of charlie as we made the 190 odd mile journey from London to Leeds.

As the train approached Wakefield, I experienced the usual nervous tension associated with arriving in enemy territory. You know something big may go off and it can be quite scary, but at the same time it is incredibly exciting. We all got off the train only to be met by a huge police presence. For some reason, they were not prepared to let a mob of drug crazed Millwall supporters drink in their town and forced us straight back onto the train.

The train pulled into Leeds and we were met by another large reception committee of boys in blue. They were not prepared to put up with any of our protests and forced us straight on to buses to Elland Road. We arrived at the ground two hours before kick-off and were not allowed to go for a drink which put a bit of a downer on the day, but we eventually entered the ground in time to see the game start.

Despite the difficulties in travelling to Yorkshire, about 1,500 Millwall supporters were there that night to offer fantastic vocal support to the players. Elland Road has always been a hostile ground to visit because the home crowd really get behind their team and the atmosphere can be quite intimidating. For once though, the Millwall players rose to the occasion and turned in a classic performance to win 2-1.

As I expected, the police got us out of Leeds without any delay after the match, and we ended up in Doncaster. There was a two hour wait for the next train to London and the police did not want us to leave the station, but after a heated discussion, we surged past them and made our way into the town. As far as I know, there was no trouble in Doncaster that night, and everyone returned to the station in good spirits. As the sleeper train pulled in, the passengers on the train were none too happy to see the platform packed with police and Millwall supporters. They weren't exactly best pleased when we got put on their train either, but they had nothing to worry about as everyone was in a party mood. It was after this game that people really started to believe that Millwall could gain promotion.

Our next away game was a mid-week game against Bournemouth. The game was immediately made all-ticket and Millwall were allocated about 2,500 tickets. This was clearly not enough to supply the demand, so Millwall agreed to show the game live on big screens at The Den. Despite not having a ticket for the game, I decided against The Den, and made my way down to the south coast, arriving in Bournemouth at about eleven in the morning.

The train was packed full of Millwall and as we got off the train and made our way into the town centre, we saw that the local traders were pulling down their shutters and shutting up shop. Pubs refused to open up and the police were on every street corner. This overreaction infuriated many Millwall who decided to get the first train out of Bournemouth so that they could enjoy a drink in nearby Poole.

I remained in Bournemouth though with cat food Paul who had already found a boozer just outside the town centre that had stayed open against police advice and was more than happy to take money from thirsty Millwall fans. I also managed to buy a ticket for the game off a Millwall tout, and when the time came, made my way to Dean Court to see the match.

Millwall won the game 2-1 after our goalkeeper had saved a penalty. It was the perfect end to a great day in a lovely town. There were no major incidents and everyone travelled home in party mood. Bournemouth do not have a large hooligan element so I think Millwall found it pretty pointless trying to start trouble. When you compare this to the mayhem Leeds fans caused a couple of years later in similar circumstances, you start to question the mentality of Leeds fans. They have long had a reputation for mindless vandalism and only seem to enjoy a fight when the numbers favour them.

On the May bank holiday, Millwall travelled to Hull knowing that a win could secure promotion to the top flight for the first time in the club's history. Thousands of Millwall fans made the long journey and were rewarded with a 1-0 victory. With other results going our way, Millwall not only secured promotion, but were actually crowned Division Two champions that day as well. Hull was overrun with ecstatic Millwall supporters who simply could not believe that the Lions would be playing First Division football next season.

The following week we were at home to Blackburn. Before the game, Les Briley was presented with the Division Two trophy and a sell out crowd went mad. Blackburn needed to win the match to get into the play-offs ahead of Crystal Palace. Millwall fans were only too happy to cheer Blackburn onto victory, thus denying Palace any chance of promotion. This was cause for a double celebration and so everyone headed onto the Old Kent Road for a right old Cockney knees up.

The atmosphere was jovial as Millwall supporters sang and danced. However, a huge police presence was starting to wind everyone up. As darkness grew and the effects of too much alcohol took over, the clashes started. A series of running battles took place and at least two pubs were seriously damaged. A police van was attacked and attempts were made to turn it over, while frightened officers cowered inside. These clashes continued throughout the night and numerous arrests were made. Shame really because there was no need for the police to be out in such numbers, and this was definitely a case of their presence actually inciting trouble that otherwise just wouldn't have happened.

CHAPTER 2

The summer of 1988 will go down in history as the second summer of love. Warehouse parties, raves, and ecstasy swept through the country. This had a knock on effect on the casual scene in football, and at the same time the police were getting much better organised to cope with the violence, and stiff penalties were being dished out by the courts, including custodial sentences. As most casuals went along to football for a laugh and a bit of excitement, this in itself was enough to put people off going to games, and many deserted the terraces and joined the rave scene.

In South East London, the talk was of Liverpool in Rotherhithe and Man United at Old Trafford. The anticipation of a first season in Division One meant that the summer just seemed to drag on despite the European Championships in Germany. When the fixture list was released, I feverishly read it and was pleased to see we had Aston Villa away on the first day of the season. I had never been to Villa Park and was looking forward to seeing the Lions make history at one of the most famous stadiums in the country.

On the day of the match, I made my way to Euston. The train into London was full of Portsmouth fans on their way to Shrewsbury, and as usual they were giving it large as they got off at Waterloo. However, when they arrived at Euston they were shocked to see hundreds of Millwall boys swarming all over the station. Much to my delight, they had to board the same train to New Street as us, and it was funny to see them sitting on the train, pretending to be invisible, when you had seen them an hour earlier boasting about what a great mob they had.

There must have been well over 3,500 Millwall at Villa Park and most could not believe their eyes as Millwall tore into Villa and went 2-0 up. The players started to believe that the First Division was going to be easy and took their foot of the pedal. By half-time, the score was level. The game finished 2-2 and the fans made their way home, eagerly anticipating the first ever Division One game at The Den against Derby County the following week.

The atmosphere at The Den was fantastic and Millwall went on to beat Derby 1-0. Points were gained at Charlton and Norwich in subsequent games and Millwall seemed to fear no one. Selhurst

Park, not for the first time, was overrun by Millwall fans who witnessed a 35 yard screamer from Sir Les Briley hit the back of the net as the Lions stormed to a 3-0 victory against Charlton. Many Lions fans also made the long trip into deepest Norfolk to see a 2-2 draw. The locals were particularly mouthy as they stood next to us in the ground, protected by a fence that went all the way to the roof of the stand. Coins were launched continually into the Millwall end as dire threats were made about what would happen to us outside.

When the game finished, however, the Norwich supporters raced out of the ground and were nowhere to be seen by the time we were let out. This quite often happens at football grounds all over the country and is something I find most annoying. Action speaks louder than words. If the Norwich fans really wanted to rip our limbs off, they could quite easily have had a go at us outside.

No doubt about it, the season had started promisingly. The team was holding its own, and the away support had been large and noisy. Most fans were looking forward to playing one of the so called big five and the first of these giants to visit The Den was Everton. Millwall had played at Goodison in a Cup tie in the mid-Seventies and quite a number of Millwall supporters were stabbed in clashes inside and outside the ground. Millwall supporters forget nothing and forgive no one, and lots of people were looking forward to getting hold of a few Scousers.

During the game it became apparent that Everton had a mob of about 40 or 50 boys in the seats in the main stand. At the final whistle, they charged through the seats in an effort to get at Millwall. The seats at Millwall that season were mainly reserved for families and so Everton's charge through them infuriated the boys on the Halfway. They could not get to Everton in the ground, but were determined to ambush the coaches on the Old Kent Road.

Within about 15 minutes of the game ending, a mob of nearly 400 had firmed up on the green opposite the Canterbury Arms. Armed with crates of milk bottles, they eagerly awaited the Everton coaches. Luckily for the Scousers, Millwall fans are not the most patient souls in the world, and when a few police vans appeared, the bottles were launched at them instead. A series of running battles ensued as the police charged Millwall off the main road and past the Carlton Tavern. Once again, Millwall had clashed with the police and had failed to get at the real enemy. They were not too downhearted though as they had seen some action and would be able to have another go at Everton later in the season.

By October, Millwall were still unbeaten home or away. Notts Forest came to The Den and with about ten minutes left they were leading by two goals. The fans were resigning themselves to seeing our proud run come to an end. Then, suddenly, John Docherty made a rare substitution and brought on Neil Ruddock. As Ruddock raced onto the pitch, he made gestures to the Halfway to get behind the team. The crowd roared and Ruddock performed like a gladiator. He inspired a fightback and Millwall pulled the game around to clinch a 2-2 draw. The noise that came from the home crowd in that period was the loudest I ever heard at The Den and must have terrified the Forest players.

The next away game I attended was at Ayresome Park at the end of October. Boro had been promoted with us the previous season and were also flying high in the league at the time. I was determined to go to this one even although I had heard that Middlesbrough was not the friendliest place to visit.

On arrival at Kings Cross, I was pleased to see a good turn out of boys and we were soon boarding the train for the long journey to Darlington. The plan was to drink in Darlington and turn up in Boro mob handed nearer kick-off time. The police were not impressed with our plan though, and would not let us out at Darlington, putting us on the local train to Boro instead. This left us with a problem as not everyone was too keen to arrive in Boro at eleven o'clock. The group split up and the main bulk of boys left the train at Thornaby, while I remained on the train with about 25 others.

As I walked out of Middlesbrough station, a local man warned me to watch my back. Boro had played Newcastle a few days earlier and a number of Geordies had been stabbed. There was a pub outside the station called De Niros and since it had only just gone eleven o'clock, the pub was empty. We went inside and settled down for the session.

I had only just ordered a pint when I noticed a couple of lads in their teens peering in through the windows. About ten minutes later, the double doors burst open and a mob of Boro lads steamed in. The 25 or so Millwall in the pub were all blokes, but I would not say they were intent on causing any trouble. The boys who had got off at Thornaby were more of a firm. Therefore, I was pleased to see Millwall instantly fight back.

Boro had attacked the pub, armed with bricks and bottles, but when you are already in a pub you have the upper hand as there is a large variety of weapons that can be used. Luckily, most of the

Millwall were around the pool table or the dart board when the pub was attacked, and armed with darts, pool balls and cues, as well as bottles and glasses, we forced Boro back out of the doors. Only a handful of Boro had actually managed to get inside the pub anyway, and they took the brunt of the counter attack from Millwall. Miraculously, no Millwall supporters were hurt.

As the last of the Boro fans left the pub, Millwall locked the doors. Boro must have had well over 50 boys outside the pub and they were desperate for us to come out and fight them. There were no police outside at the time and they must have been licking their lips at the chance of battering a few Cockneys. As I said, the Millwall supporters in the pub were not really hooligans and were not searching for trouble in Middlesbrough. When trouble found them though they were only too willing to fight back in self-defence. However, we had no intention of joining our new found friends outside and so declined the invitation to do so.

The Boro fans continued to encourage us to join them until the police turned up a few minutes later and dispersed them. After an hour or so, the police organised a bus to take us to the game and we were escorted out of the pub. A crowd of local shoppers had gathered by then, and as we were escorted onto the bus they yelled abuse at us and told us all to "piss off back to London you Cockney gobshites". Another fine example of the famed Northern hospitality you hear so much about.

Inside the ground, the atmosphere was very intense. We were in a corner and surrounded by Boro boys yelling abuse at us. The Cleveland sex scandal had recently been headline news, much to the delight of the Millwall supporters who loudly alleged that all men in Middlesbrough shag their children. Whether this is true or not, I do not know, but it incensed the locals and that was good enough for me.

Millwall lost the game 4-2 and our unbeaten run was over. It had been a long day and quite an experience. It was the first time I had been in a pub that was attacked by a football mob and it truly is a terrifying experience. I was lucky to come out of it with no injuries. Nonetheless, this did not put me off going to football or drinking in pubs before and after the games.

A couple of weeks later, there was a special report in one of the tabloid newspapers about football hooliganism. It was reported that after a recent decline in football related violence, the problem was returning to the game. As usual with the press, Millwall were used as an example of this renewed problem. It claimed that the trouble in De Niros was the worst incident of violence so far that season. Other violent incidents that were highlighted in this report also mentioned Millwall and seemed to imply that Millwall supporters were to blame for the increase in football hooliganism. I don't know whether the Boro incident was the worst that had occurred that season as I had not been involved in the countless others that had no doubt occurred at games up and down the country. I doubt very much if this investigative journalist had witnessed any of these incidents either. If he had witnessed the Boro clash, he would have seen that the Boro fans instigated it, and if anyone should be blamed for what happened that day, it should be them.

Reports similar to this regularly appear in the press and they always seem to follow the same old tired formula. Just as they thought the violence had disappeared from the game, it suddenly returns even worse than before. Millwall supporters are nearly always blamed for the resurgence in violence and are slated continually by idiotic journalists who either have no idea of what really goes on or choose to ignore the truth in order to grab the headlines and make a name for themselves.

People who do not even like football and so called "armchair" fans read these articles and religiously believe everything that is reported. Encouraged by trendy celebrities such as Nick Hancock and Paul Merton, they visualise Millwall supporters to be moronic skinheads wearing Doctor Marten boots, smashing Asian shop windows whilst under the influence of cans of super strong lager.

To a certain degree supporters of other clubs have to put up with this bullshit, but I do not think that any other group of supporters receives as much bad publicity as Millwall fans do. There are quite a few other firms just as actively violent, if not more so, than Millwall, but despite their actions, they are not tarred with the same brush on such a regular basis.

What the press fail to realise is that by reporting events such as those in Middlesbrough they are continually bolstering the reputation of Millwall supporters. Most boys who are involved in organised violence are desperate for their own particular firm to have the most violent reputation and when they are continually hearing about what a mad bunch Millwall are, they become even more determined to do Millwall in order to gain notoriety. This makes following Millwall away from home a very dangerous pastime.

A fine example of this would be our visit to Highfield Road to play Coventry in October, 1988. This was a game I was particularly looking forward to. For some unknown reason, I had always wanted to go to Coventry. As far as I knew, Coventry fans did not have a reputation for violence and I was looking forward to a relatively safe awayday.

Millwall were flying high in the league at the time, and a good three or four thousand fans made the journey. There was a pub opposite the ground which had been taken over by Millwall fans and I was enjoying a pre-match drink in a lively but friendly atmosphere.

When I got inside the ground, I saw the usual faces of the boys who made up the firm at that time. It turned out that they had been led into an ambush in the large park near to the ground. A few Coventry boys had fronted them and when Millwall charged towards them they turned around and ran away. Millwall chased them round the corner where they were confronted by a large mob of tooled up Coventry boys. A large fight started, and by all accounts Coventry got the better of it.

Obviously Millwall were not too happy about this and word soon spread around the away end. One good thing about Millwall supporters is that they do tend to stick up for each other. The fans chant "No one likes us!" and this is probably true. This leads to the Millwall fans having a siege mentality and this is why I believe that so many Millwall supporters often get involved in violent incidents. In many cases, most of the people involved have not gone to the game searching for trouble, but if they feel threatened they will stick together, and, in true South London style, offer attack as the best form of defence.

Early in the game, the Coventry boys who had been involved in the ambush turned up in the ground and took their position in the seats right next to the away fans. Millwall boys made their way to the fence and the verbal abuse soon started. Meanwhile, the game was going on and that fine sportsman, David Speedie, was playing up front for City. Speedie was always hated by opposition fans and took a lot of stick off crowds. This day was no different, and Millwall continually chanted "You Scotch cunt!", even when he was not in possession of the ball. The atmosphere was getting very hostile when all of a sudden Millwall jumped the fences and surged into the home end. The City fans backed off and the police steamed in.

Many Millwall fans were attacked and a few more were dragged out to be ejected or arrested. The bulk of the Millwall supporters were not pleased at the reaction of the police. Both sets of fans had been baiting each other, but it was the Millwall who took the beating from the police. Really, this should have come as no surprise as I find that the police usually prefer to attack the away fans rather than fans from the home team. In addition, Millwall did make the first charge. Even so, this was used as an excuse by the Millwall fans to start ripping out seats and to generally start ripping up the stand. Seats were launched at City fans and this went on for some time before order was eventually restored.

All in all, this turned out to be a surprisingly violent day. Millwall fans must take their share of the blame. Certainly, the press blamed Millwall (no surprise there, then), but the City fans and the police were far from being innocent parties. The City fans were armed and waiting for Millwall in the park. After they did well in that incident, they turned up next to the away end and were obviously wanting more trouble. When it kicked off again, I think they were surprised by the numbers that were prepared to fight. For their part, the police had let the two sets of fans sit next to each other even although they must have been aware that a serious disturbance had already occurred outside. They then steamed in to quell the trouble, but in doing so, lit the fuse for the vandalism that then went on in the stand.

In November, Millwall travelled to Anfield to face Liverpool. We had only been given a small allocation of tickets and so once again the match was shown live on big screens at The Den for those who couldn't travel. I managed to get a ticket, and on arrival at Euston found two or three hundred Millwall boys waiting to join the service train to Lime Street. One of the newsagents inside the station was selling a carpentry magazine with a free gift of a craft knife attached to the front cover. Amongst the Millwall fans that day was a large contingent of budding carpenters who were keen to purchase the magazine to obtain their free gift. This delighted the Asian shopkeeper and everyone was happy as we set off to Liverpool.

When we got to Lime Street we were literally dragged off the train by the police. The sticks were out and we were frogmarched to the end of the platform. When some of the fans questioned the heavy-handed tactics, they were physically and verbally abused by the police. The police warned us that we would all be thoroughly searched and individually photographed before being marched the two or three miles to Anfield in the drizzle. How can the police justify treating human beings like this? Most of the Millwall fans on the train were innocent fans looking forward to a drink and a football match. I have to admit that there was a firm on the train who were tooled up and looking for trouble, but even so, this does not give the police the right to deny everyone on that train their civil liberties.

I suppose the police will justify their behaviour by claiming that a number of knives were found on the ground after being discarded by Millwall prior to being searched and photographed, but once again, every Millwall supporter was blamed for the actions of the minority.

The game itself was quite memorable as Millwall took the lead and ended up gaining a well deserved point. What should have been one of the highlights of my days watching The Lions though was ruined by the Merseyside police.

The next big game was THE big one. Home to West Ham. At the time, I was regularly drinking in the Crown And Anchor pub in New Cross. This pub was always busy on matchdays, but could never be classed as a main pub. Quite a few faces did drink in there, but the main bulk of Millwall's firm was using the Carlton Tavern at the time. Although the Carlton was fairly small, it was hidden away, just off the Old Kent Road. There was a large green opposite the pub and so quite a few people could use the pub and drink outside. The main advantage of using this pub was that it was away from the prying eyes of the police on the Old Kent Road, but if any mob did stroll down the Old Kent Road looking for action, Millwall could get a decent firm together within minutes.

The Carlton was probably about two minutes walk from the Crown And Anchor. In between these two pubs are two other drinking holes, The Prince Of Windsor and The Canterbury Arms. Both of these pubs were not really used by Millwall supporters on match days at that time. On the day of the match, The Crown And Anchor was operating a members only policy. For some reason, I had not obtained a membership card and the bouncers would not let me in. There was about ten of us outside the pub trying to persuade the bouncers to let us in, but the pub was packed and there was no room inside.

Whilst we were outside the pub, we were horrified to see a mob of two or three hundred boys walking up the New Cross Road. This was about 12 o'clock, and incredibly there was only one police van in the vicinity. It was obvious this mob was West Ham and I was well aware that there was a similar amount of Millwall fans just two minutes walk away in the Carlton. With only one police van in the area it looked like I had found myself in the middle of what potentially was going to be the mother of all battles.

As the ICF approached the Crown And Anchor, I thought they would attack the pub since it was packed full of Millwall supporters locked inside. They carried on past the Crown And Anchor however, and I breathed a sigh of relief when they ignored us. They appeared to be heading towards the Carlton, but as they approached the Prince Of Windsor, they surged across the road and launched a vicious attack on the pub windows.

Ten minutes earlier I had passed the Windsor and had not bothered going in because it was virtually empty. Whatever prompted the ICF to attack an empty pub, I will never know. What I do know is that this attracted the attention of the police who converged on the mob within a matter of seconds. West Ham must have known that Millwall had a mob just around the corner. Why attack an empty pub when you could have a go at your arch rivals' main mob? Maybe they bottled it, but to be honest, I find this rather unlikely. I had witnessed this firm from very close proximity. There were many faces and very few mugs in this mob. They also had the numbers. They certainly looked capable of putting up a good fight and may well have got a real result that day. No doubt they will claim a victory anyway, but to me they let themselves down.

Some months later, this incident was shown on a documentary about the London Underground. The footage was shot from the back of a police van. The police openly admitted that they had made a mistake and had failed to prevent the ICF marching towards the Old Kent Road. The police in the van were shitting themselves as they knew it would erupt when they confronted Millwall, and they seemed as surprised as I was when West Ham chose to attack an empty pub rather than have it with Millwall.

If you watch the documentary closely, as the ICF are outside the Canterbury Arms, you will see quite a few of them looking towards the Carlton. There are also two well known Millwall faces urging them to have a go at the Carlton. It would have been an ideal place to kick it off as there are many backstreets leading towards Peckham, and it would have been very difficult for the police to control the situation had it gone off. Instead, West Ham chose to head towards the ground, where I understand they had no further problems before the match started.

Once inside the ground, there were the usual rumours that West Ham would try to take the Cold Blow Lane End. Stories like this are always flying around at big games and usually they are complete rubbish. Although most people did not think this was likely, no one was taking any chances and many of the Halfliners chose to watch the game from the Cold Blow Lane End just in case.

Throughout the game, which Millwall lost 1-0, fans in the Cold Blow Lane End were involved in serious clashes with the police. At the final whistle, the Millwall players raced off down the tunnel. At the old Den, the tunnel was at the Cold Blow Lane end of the ground rather than in the main stand. The West Ham players, as is the custom, had gone down to the away end to applaud their fans. After giving it the big one in front of their own fans, they turned round and realised that they had to walk towards the Cold Blow Lane End which was packed full of angry hyped up Millwall fans. Most of the players looked terrified and hurried into the tunnel, dodging the missiles that were being launched in their direction. Paul Ince, who seems to think he is football's equivalent to Lenny McLean, refused to show any fear at first. As he approached the penalty area he was the last player on the pitch and appeared not to have a care in the world as he strolled towards the tunnel. All that was about to change as the sky was lit by hundreds of glistening coins all aimed at his ugly head. Suddenly, the Guvnor dropped his bottle and ran into the safety of the tunnel, covering his head and looking absolutely terrified.

As we left the terrace, we saw a group of West Ham walking out of the ground behind the main stand. This group of fans had been in the seats, and to be fair they were just normal fans. This did not worry Millwall who just steamed into them and chased them back into the West Ham end. In an effort to protect this group of Irons (no pun intended), the police baton charged Millwall out of the ground and into Cold Blow Lane. A series of running battles followed until the police had dispersed the Millwall into the maze of backstreets underneath the high rise flats that lay just behind The Den.

There were numerous other clashes after the game which I did not witness so I will not comment on what actually happened. I have heard various stories, but as I was not there I do not wish to say what may have happened as I cannot guarantee the accuracy of each story. I also understand though that the trouble continued late into the night in the East End.

This appears to be quite a common situation at these games. If the game is played at The Den, the police presence is so high that the two sets of fans usually arrange to meet each other at locations well away from the match itself. This has the advantage of making it more difficult for the police to deal with. In addition, the people involved are usually main faces, people in the know, and therefore it is an opportunity for the two main firms to get it together. If someone gets run, they can't really turn around with the usual excuses that it was not the main firm or that they were attacked without warning or that there were too many Old Bill about.

Every club has their local rivals, the team that they hate the most. At most derby matches there is a highly volatile atmosphere and violent incidents are common at games such as these. Some derby games are worse than others, with The Black Country, Hampshire, and South Wales derby matches being especially violent. I usually find that derby matches that are played every year, such as Arsenal and Spurs, are not as bad as other derbies that only happen once every few years. This is not to say that it does not go off at these games - in the North London derby, for example, there is an incident of some kind at almost every game. However, the firms know each other so well that you can almost guarantee where it is going to go off and the numbers that'll be involved. The police are also clued up and are usually on hand to deal with whatever arises.

Due to the differing fortunes of West Ham and Millwall, we are only likely to play each other very occasionally, and so when the two sides do clash, you are guaranteed trouble on a large scale. I am not claiming that this match is the best, biggest or most fiercely competitive derby in England, but I do believe it may be potentially the most violent.

As an inexperienced Millwall supporter, I was fortunate in that I had already attended two derby matches against West Ham. What struck me about this particular rivalry was the fact that for so many fans from both sides, the battle on the terraces and in the streets and pubs appeared to be much more important than actually winning the game. Sure, it was great to beat the Irons on the pitch, and it annoyed me when Millwall lost, but what was really vital was to show the opposing fans that we were better than them in every respect. We had to be better dressed, we had to take more to Upton Park than they would bring to Millwall, we had to be able to confront their mob, stop them taking liberties, and send them home, fearful of ever turning up at The Den again. Victory on the terraces would be talked about long after a 2-1 win in a meaningless Cup game, that was for sure.

CHAPTER 3

In January, 1989, Millwall were drawn at home to Liverpool in the Fourth Round of the FA Cup. The game was moved to the Sunday since it was to be shown live on TV, but despite the presence of the cameras, there was a full house at The Den and most home supporters believed we were capable of winning. The game turned out to be a huge disappointment though, as once again the Lions failed to perform in a big game and Liverpool won quite comfortably. The crowd should have expected this really, but all supporters live in hope that one day the team won't let you down.

As we left the ground, it became apparent that a large mob was gathering and we all headed out to the back of The Den, near the old greyhound stadium. The Liverpool coaches were parked in the area and many Millwall were picking up stones and bricks ready to attack the Scousers as they left the ground to return to their transport home.

The police were watching this happen, but did not really have the numbers to prevent what was going on. One police officer must have seen a Millwall fan picking up weapons because he went over to the fan and tried to arrest him. Seeing that the officer was on his own, and knowing that his own mates would back him up, the fan resisted arrest. A fight started, and within seconds the officer was on the ground and was being viciously attacked by a large group of Millwall. A handful of police tried to come to his rescue, but they were heavily outnumbered by Millwall. All these police officers were attacked and when a police van rushed into the crowd, this was also attacked before the police could get out of the van. The police were really getting a hiding here. There could not have been more than 20 police trying to fight a couple of hundred Millwall, and the police had no option but to make a tactical retreat. The crowd was really hyped up by this stage, and they attacked the empty Liverpool coaches causing substantial damage.

The mob left the area and headed towards the Ilderton Road. Waiting for them on the main road was a line of riot police. They must have been aware that a few of their colleagues had been attacked and were quite keen to get some revenge. It all kicked off again and the fans were charged into the housing estate behind the

Canterbury Arms. The police certainly got their revenge in the estate that evening. Millwall may have won a battle, but the police certainly won the war.

I was with a friend from Scotland at this game and he could not believe the ferocity of the attack on the police officers. He had never seen anything like this north of the border and pointed out that when the police arrive in Scotland, the trouble usually ends there and then. Although this would be sensible, on many occasions I have seen the trouble escalate as a direct result of a police presence. The fans at Millwall have little respect for the police. The police do tend to treat every Millwall fan as a potential hooligan and this antagonises many genuine fans who have no interest in causing trouble. That said, many people appear to turn up at Millwall for big games with the sole intention of having it with the police. I don't know what the police can do about this. After all, they do have a job to do and cannot just stand by and let the fans do whatever they want. Maybe, if they treated everyone with a bit more respect and courtesy, more people would be on their side and would not be so keen to see them get attacked.

The number of police at Millwall games is still higher than average. This may well be justified by recent problems, but at the same time this police presence does encourage the siege mentality that I mentioned earlier. It's a vicious circle. The more police, the more tension. The more tension, the more violence. The more violence, the more police. And so it continues. Millwall Football Club have tried employing more stewards instead of police to keep an eye on the crowd, but if the police command little respect from the supporters, the stewards have virtually none whatsoever. They are generally regarded as sad little men who have nothing better to do on a Saturday afternoon. They tend to concentrate on petty issues like trying to force you to sit in a designated seat. Seeing as the ground is hardly ever more than half full, this can be very annoying. And when it has kicked off inside the ground, the stewards are an absolute waste of time. They do nothing to prevent people running onto the pitch. This is a vital part of their duties and if they are not doing what they are paid to do, they should be sacked. I often ask myself what kind of a man would want to become a steward. Usually, they are men who seem to get a thrill out of putting an orange bib on and ordering people about.

Although we were now out of the FA Cup, our league position was still remarkably healthy. Liverpool and Arsenal were the two overwhelming favourites to eventually win the league, but Millwall and Norwich were both in with an outside chance.

In February, we were due to meet Arsenal twice. If we could take six points from these two games, our dreams of Championship glory would come closer to reality. The first game was at The Den and was an all ticket sell out. In their usual way, Arsenal managed to kill the game and produced a highly professional performance. We left the Halfway disappointed with the Lions' performance and headed towards the Old Kent Road for an after match drink. I was not surprised to see hundreds of Millwall supporters mobbing up opposite the Prince Of Windsor.

There was a large number of police keeping an eye on this ever increasing mob when, suddenly, their vans roared off towards the ground. It was fairly obvious the Arsenal fans had now left The Den and that a mob of Gooners were on their way to meet us. We followed the police past the Crown And Anchor and down towards the Duke Of Albany. We were met by a large contingent of riot police and were chased back towards the New Cross Road. Once on the main road, we firmed up again. There must have been about 400 Millwall, but the police were not going to let us remain there. Once again they charged us towards the Canterbury Arms and into the high rise estate that lies behind this pub. They continued baton charging Millwall supporters all around this estate until such time as the large numbers had dispersed into small groups.

After being chased into a block of flats, I was captured by a group of police along with two other fans. We were searched and about to be placed in a van when the police received further orders to go elsewhere. Luckily, they abandoned us and this was our cue to get out of the estate and jump on a bus to the Elephant And Castle where we could enjoy a peaceful drink.

I then made my way to Waterloo, where I met a couple of friends. They were both Arsenal fans and had been to the game with their mob. They said that Arsenal had got a good firm together, led by one of their more infamous coloured top boys, and were making their way to meet Millwall when the police had intervened. It was therefore no real surprise that the police had been so brutal towards us. Under no circumstances were they prepared to let the Gooners and the Bushwackers play out their war games on their patch.

I expected a lot of trouble when we visited Highbury a few weeks later for an evening game. Millwall tore Arsenal apart that night, but missed chance after chance. A Les Briley stormer was controversially disallowed and the game ended 0-0. Effectively, this put us out of the Championship race and the Millwall fans were very disappointed. Although I later heard that there were a number of violent clashes after the game, I did not see any myself.

In March, we travelled to Merseyside for the game at Everton. A large mob of Millwall were on the early train to Lime Street, but as always seems to be the case with Millwall, no one could make their mind up about what we were to do on our arrival in Liverpool. By the time we got to Runcorn, we were still undecided and about 30 of us got off and went for a drink in the pub opposite the station, leaving the rest to take their chances in Liverpool.

After downing a few pints, it was finally decided that we would hire a number of taxis to take us to Goodison. A local firm, pleased with the offer of work, quickly dispatched a convoy of taxis to the pub, all driven by curly haired Scousers with a sharp sense of humour, a deep love of football, and a strong passion for their home city. I jumped in the first cab with three other lads, and Macca, our driver for the day. He kindly offered to take us to Goodison on a route that would avoid any unfriendly parts of the city. We declined his kind offer and asked him to take us to the ground via these "dodgy areas".

The convoy of cabs made their way through Toxteth, Lime Street, past the American Bar, Stanley Park, and other famous Liverpool hovels, while Macca gave us a running commentary on why Liverpool is a much more violent city than London. As we approached the ground, he warned us to avoid a pub called The Blue House as this was always packed full of Evertonians. We saw the pub as he drove by and demanded that he stop the cab. As all the cabs pulled up, the 30 of us made our way towards the The Blue House and as we did so a mob of Millwall left the pub. There were quite a few blacks amongst this mob and some of them recognised some of the lads we were with. They explained that the pub was full of Millwall and that Everton were nowhere to be seen.

I arrived at the ground and joined the shorter queue for the turnstile. When I got into the ground, I realised that the queue had been so short because it was the queue for the away terrace rather than the seats. Most Millwall boys were in the seats above us and the view from the terrace was diabolical. I spoke to a policeman and he advised me that I could transfer into the seats if I was prepared to pay the extra. To do so, I would need to leave the ground and pay the difference at the appropriate turnstile. Obeying these instructions, I left the ground and tried to hand over the extra sum to the turnstile operator. Unsurprisingly, he refused to let me re-enter the ground, and much to the delight of the laughing policemen standing there, I had to pay the full amount to get back into the ground. I later heard that the police had used this scam on a few other Millwall fans. No doubt the turnstile operator was on the fiddle too, but what the hell. These Scousers do have to make money in any way they can because of the high unemployment in the area, and they really are friendly and witty characters when you get to know them.

The game ended 1-1 and we were herded out of the ground to await buses to take us back to Lime Street. The police held back a large group of Everton fans while we waited, and they quite clearly had a few boys in this group who were eager to get hold of us. Although there was not that many police separating the rival factions, no one from either side made a charge at each other. A metal bolt was thrown into the Millwall crowd, narrowly missing my head, but even this incident did not spark any trouble. At the end of the day, I think everyone was particularly wary of the Merseyside Police who always appear to be very heavy handed, and never put up with any bollocks from away fans.

Around about this time, Millwall Football Club floated on the stock market, offering shares at 20 pence each. The minimum you could purchase was £100 worth of shares. I am no city whizzkid, but I knew that Millwall would not stay in the top flight forever, and would one day (sadly sooner rather than later) get relegated. This would have a negative effect on the price of the shares and would result in the shareholders being out of pocket. I chose not to purchase any shares.

On the 15th of April, 1989, we were due to face Liverpool at The Den, but Liverpool were in the FA Cup semi finals, so the game was postponed for a few weeks. Liverpool played Nottingham Forest at Hillsborough that day, a match that will go down in history as the day 96 football fans were killed on the terraces. It was not as a result of hooliganism though, but as a direct result of overcrowding. Anyone who has stood on the terraces has found themselves crushed from time to time, and everyone felt sorrow for the victims. The world of football was in mourning and there was talk of the following week's fixtures being cancelled as a mark of respect to the victims. In the end, the fixtures were played, but there was to be a one minute silence before each game.

Millwall played West Ham at Upton Park the week after the Hillsborough tragedy. Not really the best fixture to play so soon after the events in Sheffield because of the potential for violence. As usual, Millwall turned up in the East End mob handed and were met by West Ham. The police made 23 arrests before the game had even started as fans clashed outside the Prince Of Wales in Plaistow. The fighting continued in the streets around Upton Park, and axes, knuckle dusters, knives, and ammonia sprays were some of the weapons confiscated by the police.

Both sets of fans made their way to the ground and were preparing to observe the one minute silence. The hatred between the fans was so great that a tiny minority of fans from both sides continued to yell abuse at each other. Other fans tried to get them to shut up, but this just had the effect of making the noise louder. At the end of the minute, the bulk of the West Ham supporters chanted "Scum!" at the away end. They were quite happy to pass the blame for the lack of respect onto our shoulders, when in reality, it was a handful of idiots from both sides that had caused the damage. The reaction of the West Ham fans obviously worked though, because the following day the papers once again slagged off the Millwall supporters for their behaviour.

After the game, the police herded us to the tube station and put us on a tube to take us out of the East End. Most of the blokes on the tube were quite happy to get out of the area as they were heading back to Surrey Docks anyway where they had arranged to meet the ICF in The Warrior later on that evening. However, when the tube failed to stop at Whitechapel, the mood on the train deteriorated. By the time the tube pulled into Monument station, the supporters were ripping the carriage to bits. The emergency cord was pulled and the tube came to a stop. The doors were forced open and a mob of irate Millwall supporters surged out of the station looking for further action. There were no police around, but unfortunately there were no West Ham fans either, and so everyone walked over London Bridge and back onto their own manor.

A few of us enjoyed a drink on Borough High Street, but the majority of lads returned to Surrey Docks to wait for the arrival of the ICF. West Ham duly arrived, and as they left the station they were attacked by mobs of Millwall who had been waiting in The Warrior opposite the station. As the Irons retreated, one of them dropped an axe. This was seized by a Millwall boy and used to good effect.

The Liverpool game was rearranged and was played near the end of the season during the week. I had never been so tightly packed in at The Den, so you can imagine my surprise when it was announced that the crowd was well below capacity. This is a ploy that Millwall and quite a few other clubs appear to use quite often, probably to protect their revenue from the taxman. The atmosphere at The Den that night was not as good as it should have been with such a large crowd in attendance, and the evening was turning into a bit of an anti-climax. After the game, I went for a quick drink in the Windsor before setting off to New Cross Gate to catch my train home. I walked along New Cross Road, but as I approached the station, I noticed little groups of two or three lads loitering with intent. The strange thing was that I recognised all their faces and knew that collectively they were a firm. I decided to stick around to see what they were waiting for.

Shortly afterwards, the police escorted the Liverpool fans to the station, and as they turned out of the side street and onto New Cross Road, one bloke came charging out of the garden of a derelict house and fired a flare gun straight into the Liverpool escort. The Scousers and the police panicked while the small groups of Millwall fans firmed up and attacked the escort. This must have lasted only 30 seconds before the police got their act together and started wading into the Millwall boys who then quickly left the scene of the crime. I stayed in the area as I was catching a train from New Cross Gate, and I have to say that everyone in that escort looked absolutely petrified. It had been a vicious, premeditated attack that had been well organised. It not only surprised the Scousers, but also the police, and as far as I know no one was arrested.

The last away game of the season was at Newcastle. I was particularly looking forward to visiting St. James' Park as I had heard it was an intimidating place for London fans to visit. However, that season Newcastle had a terrible team and the fans were continually lobbying to have the board of directors sacked. Earlier in the season, Millwall had beaten Newcastle 4-0 at The Den in a game that was so easy the Newcastle fans even cheered each time we scored.

Newcastle took a good mob to Millwall that day and in the morning clashed with Middlesbrough fans at Kings Cross. Some Newcastle fans were also arrested in London when the police searched a car and found an assortment of weapons, and later these fans were to receive a custodial sentence. The Geordies were also involved in trouble with Millwall fans near The Den, and as they left the ground a few of them attacked the Directors box in an attempt to get at their own directors. All these incidents added a little edge to this game and a good mob of Millwall fans made the journey to Tyneside.

A lot of Millwall flew to Newcastle, but I took a train. Arsenal were away at Boro on the same day and the train was packed full of Arsenal fans. There was only a handful of Millwall on my train and as usual the train was delayed. We arrived in Newcastle about two o'clock to be met by a strong police presence on the platform who demanded to know where the rest of our mob were. Once we had convinced them that Harry The Dog and his mob were not hiding in the toilets, they gave us the option of a lift to the ground or they could leave us and we could take our chances in the town. The first option seemed safer and so we took our seats in the back of the police van.

The ground was virtually empty as most of the Geordies had boycotted the game as part of their protest against the way the club was being run. Various people kept invading the pitch throughout the game to sit down on the centre spot. The Millwall fans found this strange behaviour most amusing, and whenever there was a lull in proceedings we started up the chant of "Sack the board!". This was greeted with a large cheer from the home fans who would then continue with their protests.

After the game, the police walked us back to the station. Although a few locals threw some stones at us, they were soon chased away. Most of the Geordies were in the car park yelling abuse at club officials anyway, and so we left Newcastle without any major trouble.

The last game of the season saw Southampton at The Den. We finished mid-table which was more than anyone had expected at the start of the season. For most fans, this season had been the highlight of their supporting life. It had been my first full season following Millwall all around the country and I had attended about 35 games which was quite a respectable figure. It had been an eventful season and one I doubt I will ever experience again. These days, I can't envisage Millwall taking on the giants of English football week in week out and giving them all a good game. In all honesty, I would hate to see Millwall in the Premiership now anyway, as it would attract all kinds of glory boys to The Den. Therefore, I will be eternally grateful that I saw Millwall compete in the top flight when they did.

At the start of the season, the press had predicted that every Millwall game would be accompanied by scenes reminiscent of Luton in 1985. As it turned out, the police mounted a large operation at every away game and, most of the time, the press were forced to report on the football. More often than not when trouble did occur, it had been between Millwall and the police. I was not too keen on getting involved in this as you will never beat the police - they have too many advantages. If you have got the bottle to try, you have to be prepared to face the consequences and these certainly do not appeal to me.

In May 1989, I went to the match at Hampden Park between Scotland and England. It was the first time I had travelled away with England and was a day I shall never forget, for many reasons. I will not go into them now as this book is about Millwall, not England. Anyone who went to Hampden that day will know what I'm talking about anyway. Following the game though, I made my mind up that I would go to Italy in 1990 to watch England in the World Cup which gave me something to look forward to, but it meant a lot of saving up too. Therefore, I didn't plan to go to so many Millwall games in 1989/90.

The new season started with an away match at Southampton. I travelled to the South coast for that one, and had an enjoyable day out and a good drink. Despite my financial hardship, I did continue to go to most games, including the South East London derby at Crystal Palace. I always enjoy these games, but especially when they are played at Selhurst Park. Palace never bring a good support to Millwall and yet we always fill our allocation at their place. That day was no exception and as I passed through the turnstile into the Arthur Wait Stand I was in good spirits, until I was met by a volley of spit that had come from the mouth of one of the clowns who follow Palace. This came as a bit of a surprise as usually it is only bollocks that come from their mouths. If you don't believe me, just tune in to David 'Kid' Jensen.

Naturally, the offending clown was protected by a fence, but he appeared to be very keen on continuing our duel in the seats upstairs. Inside the stand, the Palace fans were being their usual mouthy selves, but Millwall were not prepared to put up with it. As the players raced onto the pitch to the tune of *Glad All Over*, we broke through the police line and steamed straight into our rivals. The game itself was a classic, but as usual Palace sneaked a lucky victory.

The Irons had been relegated the previous season, but had been replaced by Chelsea and so this became *the* game for the Millwall boys. I dare say a few Chelsea fans were also looking forward to it. The first game was at Stamford Bridge, and in the week leading up to the game rumours were flying around that someone had managed to obtain hundreds of tickets for the West Stand. The tickets were to go on sale in the Crown And Anchor on the Friday night. Plenty of Millwall were waiting in the Crown for the arrival of the tickets, but it came as no real surprise to anyone when the tickets failed to materialise.

On Saturday morning, we mobbed up in The Fort in Bermondsey. This was a heavy mob with lots of old faces and I felt quite happy as we set off for Stamford Bridge. We hopped on a bus to the Elephant where we met another huge mob of Millwall who had been drinking in the Charlie Chaplin. By the time we arrived at Sloane Square, there must have been a good 400 of us. Our numbers were swelled by another mob of Millwall who were drinking in a pub opposite Sloane Square. Pleased with the size of our mob, we set off along the Kings Road. A mob of about 70 Chelsea came out of a pub to confront us, but soon backed off when they saw our numbers. A few idiots began singing and smashing shop windows, but they were soon put in their place by the main boys.

Once we arrived near the ground, the fun really started. There were plenty of Chelsea fans hanging around and most of them were throwing missiles at us. By this time, we were under heavy police escort, but every now and then a few Millwall managed to break out of the escort and steam into Chelsea. This was not Chelsea's main mob we were up against though, it was mainly their beer monsters. They put up a brave fight, but really didn't stand a chance. A lot of Millwall were not really that interested as they were only after the main Chelsea boys and everyone knew they would be around somewhere.

Millwall lost the game 4-0, but to be fair, we played really well. We missed chance after chance, but every time Chelsea attacked, they scored. When they scored their fourth goal, it was too much to take for some of the 5,000 Millwall fans and a few surged through the open doors in the fences at the bottom of the terrace. They charged onto the running track, but the police managed to prevent a full scale pitch invasion. One fan ran onto the track, punched a copper in the face, and ran straight back onto the terraces, much to our amusement. Despite their best efforts, Chelsea were unable to get on the pitch and so most of their firm left the ground to wait for us outside. We were kept inside the ground for about an hour and became so angry at the delay in our exit, that some Millwall fans burnt down a Save The Bridge hoarding.

Eventually we left the ground and were escorted to the underground station at Fulham Broadway. The police had managed to clear the Chelsea fans from the surrounding streets, but most Millwall knew where they could be found and left the tubes at the earliest opportunity to return to West London. A series of running battles then ensued in the Kings Road, Sloane Square and Earls Court areas. The fighting went on for hours and by the end of the day the police had made 35 arrests on top of the 50 fans ejected from the ground.

Apart from the football, it had been a great day out and the talk amongst the Millwall fans was of the return game at The Den on the final day of the season. As Christmas approached and Millwall sank into the relegation zone, it became apparent that Chelsea could relegate us that day. The game had even more potential for serious disorder.

CHAPTER 4

The defeat at Chelsea typified our season. We had started promisingly, but it was obvious to everyone that we lacked the sufficient quality in depth to sustain another season in the top flight. We had outplayed Chelsea, quite comprehensively in my opinion, yet still we suffered a 4-0 defeat. The fans were expecting relegation and seemed quite prepared to face the consequences - after all, they were quite used to lower league football. All we asked was for our players to give 110% commitment in each game and fight for the pride of the team. With players like Hurlock, Rhino, and Briley, you had no doubt that we would not go down without a fight. Other players, Sherringham in particular, appeared to believe that they were top quality players and deserved to stay in this league on merit alone.

With hindsight, it may seem stupid to criticise Teddy as in later years he did go on to perform at the very highest level. In 1989/90, he was not the same player he was in 1995/96 though, and he took a lot of stick from many Lions fans. It is fair to say that Sherringham was most certainly not the fans' favourite come the end of the 1989/90 season.

With the threat of relegation looming, Christmas 1989 was not the most happy of holidays. However, Millwall had been drawn away to Man City in the Third Round of the Cup and a lot of fans were looking forward to making the journey to Manchester.

Once again, Euston was mobbed by eight o'clock on the Saturday morning. When you set out for big games up north, it is always a great relief when you bump into other Millwall fans in London early in the morning. As you go up the escalators onto the concourse at Euston, it always fills your heart with pride to see a mob of 200 or so like minded people. Straight away, any fears you may have about the day ahead are lifted and you know that you are going to have a good day.

I was travelling with Andy, an old mate from school, and we managed to sneak some drink onto the train and settled down for the long journey ahead. Once we had been on the train for an hour or so, the drink and the early start finally caught up with us and both of us nodded off to sleep.

When we finally woke up we were greeted by the sight of a line of police vans and dogs at Manchester station. We wiped the sleep from our eyes and looked down our carriage. When we left Euston, the train had been packed with some good boys and I was quite happy with this as I did not fancy going into Moss Side with just my friend for company. However, the train was now virtually empty. There was about 15 of us who got off the train and one of them explained to me that most of the Millwall fans had got off at Stockport and were planning on making their way to Maine Road direct from Stockport, thus avoiding the police presence in Manchester. No doubt they had a few other things planned, but my main concern now was myself.

The police rounded up the small number of Millwall present and asked where the rest of our boys were. We denied any knowledge of seeing any other Millwall fans on the train, but the Manchester police must have received a call from Euston giving them an idea of the number of supporters on the train so weren't taken in by our porky pies. The funny thing was that there was a line of buses ready to take the fans to the ground. As it was only 10:30 in the morning this was a bit of a liberty and would have ruined the day for everyone.

The police by this time were in a bit of a panic. I dare say they had to justify to their Chief Inspector why they had so many police on the platform, with dogs and vans and all those buses to meet little more than a dozen innocent people. For a while the police were going to keep us in the station until they found the rest of the Millwall, but eventually they relented and let us leave.

We found a pub in the centre of Manchester and later on took a cab to Moss Side. 4,000 Millwall fans watched a boring 0-0 draw in a volatile atmosphere. It turned out that after having a drink in Stockport, a good mob of Millwall had turned up in Moss Side and had took liberties with quite a few of the locals.

At the end of the game, the police escorted Millwall round the back of the Kippax side terrace and into the car park, and fans who had travelled on club transport were escorted to their buses. I asked a few police officers what they were going to do with the fans who had travelled up on the service trains, like walk us back to Piccadilly or put us on buses, but the police did not seem to know what their plans were. My own plan centred around not really wanting to make my own way back to Piccadilly as I was well aware of the risks.

45

After half an hour or so, the bulk of the Millwall support had left the area, leaving about 25 of us in the car park. The police appeared to be about to leave us on our own too and most of us were not happy. This was not a firm of lads, this was a group of 25 or so people, some as young as 15. No one wanted any trouble and no one wanted to put themselves at risk by walking two or three miles through one of the most notorious housing estates in the country.

After receiving no help at all from the police, we really had no choice but to leave the car park and head into Moss Side. None of us had a clue what way to go, but this turned out not to be a problem. After about two minutes we were approaching the end of the road, when a huge mob of Man City fans came charging round the corner. This mob was mainly black lads and quite a few were tooled up with baseball bats. Without hesitation, we turned and ran back towards the car park. Luckily, the police were still there and as we stopped running, they came over towards us. "Are you the Cockney bastards that are causing trouble?", one police officer politely asked.

When I explained that we had been chased by a gang of blacks armed with baseball bats, he just laughed and replied, "Well, that's what you came here for. Go and fight them if you think you are so hard."

Other police made similar comments to other people and not one policeman offered to help us get back to Manchester city centre. The police had basically set us up, knowing some of us could have been killed. Eventually, one of the fans went up to a copper on a motorbike and told him that he was going to kick him off his bike and smash the bike to bits. The copper explained that he would be arrested if he did this, but as this seemed healthier than walking into a mob of Mancs armed with baseball bats, he didn't really care. By now, the police were beginning to realise that we would not be going anywhere without them and started to take the situation a little more seriously.

We were eventually put in the back of some police vans and driven to Piccadilly station. The police were laughing at us, saying we got what all Cockneys deserve when they try to come fighting in Manchester. We ignored their childish and ill-informed opinions. All of us knew the truth and we did not need to justify ourselves to these little men who only become powerful when they put on a uniform. I knew that one day they would see Millwall batter the cowardly Mancs who can only attack you when they have the numbers and weapons behind them. The Mancs and their police are not quite as hard as they like to believe.

They dropped us outside Piccadilly and sped off, leaving us to walk up the ramp and into the station. There were quite a few dirty teenage Mancs hanging around the station, probably hoping to mug some innocent Millwall fan. They were staring at us and trying to intimidate us, but this didn't work as I for one refuse to be intimidated by some greasy Manc with a thin line of hair above his lip. Why do young Mancs always try to grow an old style Kevin Webster moustache? Do they really think it makes them look harder, older, or more attractive to female Mancs? I do not know the answer, but I do know that it makes everyone in the South laugh at them, especially when you take into consideration the clothes these idiots wear.

We marched straight up to one of the Mancs and enquired, "What number was it?"

This baffled the Manc, who replied, "Ugh?"

"The bus that rammed into your ugly boat!"

Before anything else could happen, the Manc dropped his bottle and scurried off out of the station.

My friend and I mulled over the day's events on the train journey home. It had been quite scary at times, but now that we were safe, we felt fine. We laughed at our stupidity for falling asleep on the journey up and wished that we had stayed with the mob who had caned the Mancs before the game. After a second replay, we eventually beat them to progress into the Fourth Round. This turned out to be a huge disappointment though as we then lost at Cambridge.

Our Cup run over, we were left to concentrate on our battle against relegation. In February, we faced a six-pointer against fellow relegation candidates, Manchester United, at the Den. I went to the game with a close friend who was a keen Man United fan. We spent the lunchtiine drinking in the Carlton Tavern and ended up getting slaughtered. At one stage, the pub emptied as there was a rumour that a mob of United were in the Canterbury Arms. I do not know if this was true or not because I was too far gone to take any notice. I eventually got to the ground at about twenty past three and all I could think about was drinking more lager. We left before half-time and returned to the Gibraltar pub in the Elephant And Castle.

We carried on boozing all night, and in the morning I realised I had no idea what the final score was. It turned out that United had won 2-1 and Millwall were now in dire trouble. The following week,

47

John Docherty was sacked. I often wonder whether Alex Ferguson would have been sacked if we had won that game. If so, it could have changed the course of football in the Nineties as I am sure United would not have been so successful without Fergie at the helm.

I felt Millwall were a little harsh in their treatment of John Docherty. He had performed miracles to get Millwall into the top flight and that in itself should have been enough to justify a little loyalty. With little financial support from the chairman, Reg Burr, we were never seriously in a position to remain in that league. Burr however seemed to think that Millwall were now a formidable force in the world of football and started to say that we would have to build a stadium to match our new found supremacy. News of the proposed death of The Den did not go down well with the fans, and the chairman started to take a lot of abuse.

Following John Docherty's sacking, Bob Pearson was promoted to caretaker manager. He was unable to halt the slide or prevent Tony Cascarino deserting the sinking ship for a lucrative move to Aston Villa. Despite the quality of the football, I was still determined to enjoy life in the top division. Most Millwall fans had waited a lifetime to watch Millwall play in Division One, and in all honesty, most people were just happy to be there for an extra year. No one had given us a chance the previous season and yet we played really well throughout. So to have another year in Division One was a real bonus and something to be appreciated even though relegation was only to be expected come May, 1990.

In the spring of 1990, we faced local rivals Crystal Palace at The Den. It was a beautiful Spring day, the sort of day made for watching football. As usual, we had a good drink in the Windsor before watching the game, but afterwards we decided to go into the West End for a drink. We caught a train to Charing Cross and tried to leave the station, but there was a huge police presence in and around the station and they were not letting anyone out. The police looked very flustered and smoke could be seen billowing up The Strand as the noise of police sirens echoed around the station. It seemed we had walked into a major incident, but we could not make out who was involved. It seemed unlikely that Millwall or Palace would have a mob here and we were asking ourselves who else was playing in London that afternoon.

We managed to sneak out of the station and looked down towards Trafalgar Square where we could see hundreds of riot police forming a line outside the South African embassy from where the smoke was billowing out. It soon became apparent that this was not a football incident at all. The people involved in the trouble were all filthy, scruffy, unwashed new age types who had come to the capital city to protest about the poll tax. There were many women with them and they appeared to be just as aggressive as the men, and just as ugly too.

We decided to leave the unwashed people to it and headed up to Covent Garden for a drink. As we walked up to Covent Garden, there were mobs of dirty people all over the West End and the damage to the shops and parked cars was scandalous. The police were taking a lot of stick from the protesters, but did not seem willing to retaliate. Had it been mobs of football hooligans throwing bottles and attacking police, the police would have been well up for it, but they seemed to be holding back against these lefties. Maybe this was because it was politically incorrect to kick fuck out of new age protesters - after all, you can imagine the outcry from the likes of the Socialist Workers Party about police brutality. However, no one is prepared to stick up for football fans who are often the victims of police violence, and for years we have had no alternative but to accept it as part and parcel of going to football. Now that football has become trendy among the middle classes, some politicians have latched on to this in an effort to be seen as football friendly. Although the right noises were made by David Mellor and the like following the blatant police brutality in Porto and Rome against Man United and England fans respectively, nothing has actually changed - as events in Marseilles during the last World Cup clearly showed.

We walked all around the West End trying to find a pub away from these dirty people. As I walked up a side street near Oxford Street, I saw a mob of lefties smashing some shop windows. One of the shops was a suit shop and so the lefties decided against looting anything from it. They continued their wrecking spree up Oxford Street, but as I walked past the suit shop I saw what I believed to be a man lying unconscious on the floor, surrounded by glass. I rushed up to the injured man to try to drag him away from the glass only to find he was a dead weight. As I turned him over, I saw the blank expression of a shop dummy staring back at me.

We ended up in a pub near Euston where we met a mob of well dressed black lads armed with a map of the West End and a number of empty bags. They asked us if we knew where the Armani shop was. As we were giving directions, they asked us if the lefties had already looted it. Judging by the appearance of the lefties, I very much doubted it and so waved the black lads on their way. We had a few more beers and then went home regretting our decision not to join the black lads in a spot of looting.

Man City visited the Den near the end of the season on the same day The Happy Mondays were playing a concert in London. City brought a huge mob to London that day as many of them wanted to have it with Millwall before listening to the new sound of Manchester music that night. Not only do Mancs think they are trendier than Londoners, but they also think the Manchester music scene is more happening. Dream on lads, you'll never beat the capital at anything. All the good foreign players who are now attracted to the Premier League wish to play for London teams rather than Man United, simply because London is a much better city all round. The only foreigner who actually enjoyed his time in Manchester came from Georgia, where it is common to queue for an entire day just to buy a loaf of bread. No wonder he thought Moss Side was a fantastic place to be. Even those two idiots from Oasis moved to London as soon as they could afford to.

After losing to Derby, Millwall found themselves relegated and so the final game of the season was rather pointless from a footballing point of view. However, seeing as the game was against Chelsea, local pride was at stake and it was a match that had been eagerly anticipated by both sets of fans.

It was another scorching day, so I decided to drink in the Carlton Tavern before the game as I knew that you could drink in the park opposite the pub. As the lunchtime session progressed, there were a good couple of hundred Millwall lying around on the grass, getting drunk and soaking up the rays. The atmosphere was very mellow.

At about two o'clock, I noticed that the police presence had suddenly increased quite considerably. They looked very apprehensive, as if something was happening which they did not want us knowing about. This alerted everyone, and people began to drink up, retaining their bottles for possible future use.

Word soon spread that a number of different firms of Chelsea were coming down the Old Kent Road towards the pub. A large roar went up and everyone left the park to confront Chelsea on the Old Kent Road. The police tried to block us and were met by a hail of bottles and glasses. At this stage, it was only a thin line of police, and just behind them you could see part of the Chelsea mob on the

Old Kent Road. Millwall battled desperately with the police in an attempt to reach Chelsea, but the police held their line and prevented us from breaking through.

The Chelsea mob that was visible did not appear to be making much of an effort to break out of their escort. This was rather surprising as they had a good chance to get at us. What was the point of taking the effort to come down the Old Kent Road if you don't bother doing anything when the opportunity arrives. This part of the mob must have been the idiots that are always attracted to football mobs, but everyone knew that their main boys were in the area and so Millwall were desperate to escape from the police to find them.

The police had managed to prevent us getting on to the Old Kent Road and they were now backed up by a large number of reinforcements. They baton charged us down Asylum Road and back into the park opposite the Carlton. This was a huge mistake as it meant that Millwall could tool up with all the weapons that had been thrown earlier. Once again, the bottles and glasses were launched at the police and one officer was dragged from his horse and attacked by a group of Millwall who had spotted him attacking a Millwall fan. Luckily for him, his colleagues rushed in to save him from getting seriously hurt.

Fuelled on by the alcohol and a strong desire to get at Chelsea, Millwall kept on coming back at the police every time they baton charged us. This was the most ferocious violence I had witnessed between the police and Millwall fans since the Cup game against Liverpool. This was probably even more serious, as on this occasion the police were present in large numbers and were well organised.

As is always the case, the police did eventually restore order and small groups of tired and injured Millwall fans made their way to the ground. The atmosphere in the ground was not as volatile as expected, and the Lions went down 3-1 with Kerry Dixon grabbing a hat-trick.

I expected more trouble after the game, but as far as I know the police managed to escort Chelsea out of South East London without further incident. This was enough for me and I spent the rest of the day drinking around Walworth, looking forward to Italy in the summer. For some Millwall boys though, the season was far from over and a mob of 20 or so decided to go looking for further action. They were on their way to Victoria when they bumped into a mob of Man City fans on the underground. After seeing them on their way home to Rainsville, they continued over to Victoria where they attacked The Stage Door and two other pubs often used by Chelsea. After doing what they had to do, they left the area in taxis before the police had time to arrive on the scene.

Having followed England in the World Cup and returned home from Italy, I was looking forward to the start of the 1990/91 season. Bruce Rioch had been brought in as manager, and on paper we looked to have a good team. Teddy Sherringham had agreed to stay with us and help us fight to get back to Division One. This loyalty has never been forgotten by anyone at Millwall. He had not had the best of seasons in 1989/90, and maybe he wanted to show the supporters what he was really like.

When the fixtures were announced, I was pleased that we were away at Watford as you can always have a good drink up there and there is rarely any trouble. The big day was still a few weeks away so I kept busy by enjoying the rest of the summer. I had started seeing a girl and had arranged to go out with her on the Friday. A few days before the date I received a phone call from a friend who told me that Millwall were playing a pre-season friendly against Hibernian on Friday night and the talk in Edinburgh was that Hibs were going to bring a huge mob to London, intent on taking on the famous Millwall. They already claimed to be the best firm in Scotland and doing Millwall at The Den would only enhance their reputation. I had no intention of going to the game, and felt my appearance would make no difference as to what might happen anyway. If Hibs did bring a firm down, I felt they would find little opposition from Millwall because nobody rated the game, and I had this bird to meet in any case.

Generally speaking, Millwall fans have little interest in anything Scottish. This is despite the fact that Millwall FC was founded by Scots, play in blue, and have a lion on the club badge. Scottish players are often abused and no one takes a blind bit of notice of what goes on north of the border. Had Millwall been playing Celtic or Rangers, a large crowd would have turned up, but Hibs at home on a Friday night in a friendly did not interest many people, and as it turned out the crowd was only about 3,000, including a good away following from Edinburgh.

I went out on my date and spent the evening listening to the girl tell me how everyone thought she looked like Linda Lusardi. Everyone that is apart from me. Not for the first time, I found my mind wandering towards The Den instead of concentrating on the girl I was with.

The following morning I woke up (on my own I hasten to add) and went down to the paper shop. Instantly, I noticed a small report about violent clashes on the Old Kent Road between Hibs and Millwall fans. I could have kicked myself. I was so annoyed with myself for going on a poxy date when I should have been at The Den, helping to protect our ground from hordes of drunken Scottish louts. In reality, I was well aware that my presence would have made no difference and I probably would have got a good hiding had I been involved in the disturbances. Most people would prefer to be on a date with a "Linda Lusardi" lookalike than be at the mercy of 200 Scots, but to me this was not the point. I knew something might happen and I had chosen to let my side down. I vowed that I would never let this happen again.

I do not know exactly what happened that night because obviously I was not there. I heard that a mob of Hibs turned up and smashed up the Crown And Anchor. Word soon spread around the area and a mob of Millwall got together and had a go back at Hibs. It all went off between the two sets of fans, and by all accounts Hibs got a result. Fair play to Hibs. They did bring a big mob that turned up and did what they had to do. Since that game, they have continuously bragged about their achievement. What they fail to realise is that the game was a pointless non-event and hardly any Millwall boys had any interest in it. When it did kick off, Millwall got a small but game firm together and had quite a good go back at Hibs. This was Hibs' top firm against a rag bag of Millwall who got together in minutes and still managed to have a go. One thing for sure is Millwall will never underestimate Hibs again, and should we ever meet again, under any circumstances, then the famous Hibs casuals may get to face a real mob.

CHAPTER 5

The new season finally arrived and we drove to Watford and parked the car on the other side of the town, away from Vicarage Road. As we started walking into the town in search of a pub, we asked two girls how far the ground was. Instead of giving us directions, they took us to their car and drove us to Vicarage Road. These girls were very hospitable to say the least, and we arranged to meet them later on that night in a pub in Leighton Buzzard.

We spent all lunchtime in the pub by the ground, The Red Lion (I think), and watched Millwall win 2-1 thanks to two goals by Malcolrn Allen. After a few more pints we decided to find the car and drive over to Leighton Buzzard to meet the girls, but it soon became apparent that we had no idea where the car was parked. We had been given a lift from the car to the ground and neither of us had taken any notice of our surroundings. We stumbled around aimlessly for about two hours, unable to find the car, when our search was interrupted by a ferocious thunderstorm. This was the signal for us to shelter in a nearby pub until the rain stopped. About an hour later, we left the pub even more pissed than when we had first darkened its doors, and after another hour or so we miraculously located the car.

After hugging each other in joyous celebrations, more reminiscent of the Hull away game than Watford away, we drove over to Leighton Buzzard to meet the girls. The problems continued as both of us had forgotten the name of the pub in which we were to meet them. We assumed that there would not be many pubs in Leighton Buzzard and we would try each one until we found the girls. This was not quite the case. Leighton Buzzard is near to a military base and there were loads of pubs in the town centre, all packed full of drunken squaddies. We stumbled from pub to pub, staring at all the girls, but by now I was so drunk that I would have been unable to recognise our supposed dates for the night even if we had chanced upon them. Needless to say, we never found the girls and somehow we managed to drive home without crashing the car or getting arrested. Even so, it had been an eventful day and one which truly sticks out in my mind.

I continued to attend most home games, but had decided to stop going to so many away games. I had enjoyed watching England in the World Cup in the summer so much that I chose to travel to England away games as much as I could instead. In October, 1990, I went to Dublin to watch England take on Ireland in a 1992 European Championship qualifying match and that meant some serious saving on my part.

My routine for the home games had also changed. The Prince Of Windsor had become one of the main pubs used by the boys and I would usually spend most lunchtimes in there. I had met a few Millwall boys in Italy and they also drunk there. Although we would always say hello and have a chat, I usually stayed drinking with the friend or friends I had travelled with. The drinking sessions became heavier and heavier, and this became the main reason for going to football on Saturdays. Most match days would involve getting drunk before the game, stumbling in to the Halfway after kick-off, and leaving before the end. We would then return to The Prince Of Windsor for a few more, and then move on to the Elephant for a few more before going to Waterloo and jumping on the train home.

This routine continued for all home games until we played West Ham, just before Christmas. I knew this game would be quite lively and so I wanted to keep my wits about me rather than just get drunk. The Prince Of Windsor was supposed to be shut before the game, but everyone knew that if you knocked on the back door you would be let in if you were recognised. Four of us travelled to this game, including a friend from Edinburgh who had moved down to Streatham, and we had arranged to meet another friend in the Windsor at 12 o'clock. He was one of the lads I had met in Italy and it was fair to say that he was regarded as one of the main faces at Millwall.

The four of us were let in the back door of the Windsor and after getting served we sat down in one of the corners. There were about 15 Millwall in the pub and none of them recognised us. To be honest, I was the only one out of the four of us who regularly used the pub and so these wary looks were quite understandable. We were starting to get a little nervous when the back door opened and in walked the bloke I had arranged to meet. He walked straight over to our table and explained that everyone was drinking in one of the back street pubs, just off the New Cross Road. I knew where the pub was, but as we had just got fresh pints in, I arranged to meet him there after we had finished our drinks. He left the pub and after his departure, the mood in the pub changed. The other 15 lads in the pub now knew we were sorted, and a few of them came over for a chat and apologised for giving us the evils.

We strolled down to the Fox And Hounds and made our way to the bar. The pub was packed with some of the most unsavoury characters you could ever wish to meet. It looked more like a police identification parade than a pub full of football supporters. At one stage, I didn't think the barmaid would serve me as I did not have a scar running down my cheek. As a result of the incident with the Hibs fans, the Scottish lad was scared to talk in case anyone assumed he was a Hibs fan, and one of the others had to go to the bar for him to shout his round. Of course, he may just have been nervous about opening his wallet and buying a round because of his Scottish nature.

We got chatting to a group of lads in the bar and it soon became obvious it was going to go off big style today. The reason for using this pub was because rumour had it that the ICF were going to come through Peckham. If this turned out to be true, we would quite easily be able to ambush them from here. In addition, there were quite a few other pubs in the area packed full with Millwall boys.

All this news relaxed us and we began to enjoy the drink. A bottle of amylnitrate was passed around, and much to the delight of everyone in the pub, one of my mates took a swig rather than a sniff of it. He ran off to the toilets to wash his mouth out while everyone laughed at him.

At around two o'clock, the police surrounded the pub and ordered the landlord to stop serving. Everyone left the pub and made their way to New Cross Road. All the other pubs had also been forced to shut early. To me this seemed a stupid move by the police as you now had about 1,000 Millwall fans out on the streets with nothing to do for an hour before kick-off. Naturally, someone suggested we go looking for West Ham and everyone started to make their way towards Peckham, going away from The Den. This confused some people and a number of arguments started. Some people were saying we should go to Peckham, others were saying we should go to New Cross Gate. In the end, we split up and I went with the mob towards New Cross Gate.

We headed towards the station via the back roads and as we got nearer, I realised that our mob had reduced to about 20 lads. As we turned the corner into another street, we walked straight into a mob of about 400 West Ham who were being escorted by the police from the tube station to the ground.

They spotted us straight away and broke through the police line to get at us. Amazingly, and rather stupidly, none of us turned to run and we actually stood our ground. We should have got a hell of a kicking, but luckily the police surrounded us and prevented the West Ham getting to us. As the police herded the West Ham fans back into their escort, we made a hasty retreat. When we turned the corner by the Royal Archer pub, I was relieved to see the rest of the Millwall boys streaming down the street. Excitedly, we told them that there was a large mob of West Ham in the street just one minute away. We all charged down the road that ran parallel to where West Ham were. In between these two roads were a number of connecting side streets and as we passed one of these side streets, we heard a deafening roar.

Once again, West Ham had broken away from their escort and were now charging towards us. Without hesitation, hundreds of Millwall charged up the street to confront the Irons. I think West Ham were surprised by the huge number of boys Millwall had in this mob. Although West Ham had a good 400 or so, which is a good mob in itself, Millwall easily doubled this tally and this small side street was soon alive with the sound of fighting. The police were outnumbered and were powerless to prevent the two mobs clashing. Bottles and bricks were hurled by both sets of fans, but after a brief and violent confrontation, West Ham were forced to retreat. They had no answer to the huge numbers of Millwall.

Small pockets of West Ham and Millwall fans continued to clash with each other in other side streets leading to the ground. The sound of sirens was becoming increasingly louder as more and more riot police converged on the scene. As we approached the ground, another full scale confrontation seemed likely. This time, the police had done their homework though, and hundreds of Old Bill were in position between the two sets of warring fans. Missiles continued to be launched at each other, while the police slowly but surely forced West Ham into the ground. Once the bulk of Irons were safely inside, the police then pushed Millwall towards the ground.

When we got into the Halfway, we were pleased to see that kick-off had been delayed. It was announced over the tannoy that the reason for this was because of crowd congestion in the streets outside the ground. We all laughed at this excuse as everyone knew that this was not strictly true. The mood started to turn to anger though when the tannoy announcer thanked the West Ham fans for their good behaviour outside. Everyone in that ground knew the reason for the delay was due to the ferocious fighting outside. West Ham fans had been equally responsible for this violence so why should they be thanked by an employee of Millwall Football Club? West Ham had become a little unstuck outside because of the sheer volume of Millwall fans willing to fight them, but nonetheless, they had instigated the trouble by charging at Millwall. If it was not for the fact that we had such a result outside, this thoughtless comment could quite easily have provoked further trouble inside the ground.

The game itself ended 1-1, but the day was far from over. After the game we made our way to The Warrior, opposite Surrey Docks station. We felt sure that West Ham would pop in for a drink on their way back to East London. The Warrior was packed by the time we got there and so we chose to drink in another pub just around the corner. After a couple of hours of drinking, I decided enough was enough and decided to go home. The area was still alive with Millwall, but I don't know if any further incidents occurred.

350 police had been on duty that day, and yet for the second consecutive Millwall - West Ham match, they still managed to bungle the police operation. It was reported that 13 people had been arrested and another 13 hospitalised. The News Of The World claimed that 4,000 people, some wearing gumshields, had fought a violent battle for 15 minutes before the game. I do not know whether this is an accurate number and I certainly did not see anyone wearing a gumshield, but I do know that this was the largest, longest and most violent incident I have ever been involved in at a Millwall match. On this occasion, Millwall certainly got the better of West Ham. There was an awesome mob that day that were well up for it. West Ham had turned up in large numbers and had attempted to do the business. They did not stand a chance because of the numbers we had, but to be fair, I do not think anyone could have done Millwall that day.

Millwall are quite capable of getting a mob of this magnitude for most high profile home games. However, what usually happens is that they split up and it ends up that there are a number of smaller mobs all getting up to mischief. This day was different because the police went round all the pubs and forced everyone out onto the street at the same time. It was a stupid decision to make and one which had definite repercussions. Whoever authorised this decision really needed their head examining.

The season continued with Millwall looking a good bet for promotion. I continued attending most home games and a few away games, but was involved in no further violent clashes. In April, 1991, though we faced West Ham in the return game at Upton Park. The police had decided to move the game to a 12 o'clock kick-off on the Sunday and to make it all ticket. In addition, all the pubs within the proximity of Upton Park were to be closed all lunchtime.

I did not have a ticket for the game, but decided to take my chance with a tout. I knew Millwall were mobbing up early in the morning at Surrey Docks before heading over to a pub in Stratford. Apparently, someone knew the landlord and he had promised to open up. My plans went pear shaped after a particularly heavy night on the lager on Saturday. I overslept and missed the meet at Surrey Docks. I did not know the name of the pub in Stratford and decided not to bother going all the way over there on the off chance. So, me and a mate, both ticketless, made our way to Upton Park in an attempt to secure two tickets for the Millwall end. All the touts were Irons and because the pubs were all shut, the area around the ground was packed with West Ham boys looking out for Millwall.

It did not seem sensible to ask the touts for away end tickets and I really did not want to watch the match surrounded by a bunch of Irons. As kick-off approached, we decided to leave the area and try to find a pub that was open. We ended up walking all the way over to Plaistow before finding a pub that would let us in the side door. After a few hours we made our way home without any problems. It turned out to be a very quiet day. Millwall had lost the game 3-1 and as far as I know there was no serious trouble. At long last, the police seemed to have got their act together.

A few weeks later, we played at Portsmouth in a mid-week match. Me and a mate took the afternoon off work, caught the train to Portsmouth Harbour, and spent the afternoon drinking in the pub opposite the station. The pub was fairly busy with Millwall supporters and we all decided to order cabs to take us to Fratton Park. Just before the cabs turned up, one of the Millwall boys followed a lad into the toilets. I had noticed this lad at the bar and he seemed to be taking a lot of notice of what was being said. When the Millwall boy came out of the toilet, he jumped into the first cab and left the area. He believed this bloke was an undercover copper and he had attacked him in the toilet, giving him quite a good kicking.

The cabs dropped us on the main road, leading from Fratton station to the ground. Every time I have been to Portsmouth there have always been little groups of locals in the area looking out for away fans. Tonight was no different, and it was quite a dodgy walk to the ground. We had tickets for the game, but the tickets were for the home seats, opposite the main stand. The game finished 0-0, but the night was so foggy you could barely watch the football anyway.

After the game, the two of us walked back to Fratton station. Before catching our train, we decided to go and get something to eat from the chip shop just down the road from the station. As we crossed over the road, a mob of eight or nine lads surrounded us. "Where are your boys?" they enquired.

We said that we did not know, but if they wanted a row they should go and find Millwall's mob. One of these brave lads stepped forward and said, "We have found you now, come down the alley."

Knowing he could not lose the fight, he fearlessly walked towards the alley expecting one of us to follow him. We tried to turn away and one of the other lads threw a pathetic right hander which connected with my mate's nose, causing no damage at all. We ran out of the way and down towards the station, while the Portsmouth lads accused us of being runners.

We ran onto the platform where we bumped into the Millwall fans who had been escorted back to the station. One of the lads recognised me and asked me what had happened. After telling our story, we soon got a firm together of about 25 lads and left the station in search of the Pompey boys. Unfortunately, the police found us before we found Pompey. It would have been interesting to see the reaction of the Pompey boys when faced with a real mob instead of two innocent fans. I am sure they would not have been as brave as they had been earlier.

Millwall failed to secure automatic promotion and so we faced the lottery of the play-offs for the first time. Notts County, Middlesbrough, and Brighton were the other three teams involved and we had to face Brighton in the first game. The first leg was at the Goldstone Ground. Fearful of trouble, the police moved the game to a 12 o'clock kick-off time on a Sunday morning. I fail to understand the reasoning behind this decision because all it meant was that Millwall would travel to Brighton on Saturday for the night out before the game.

Four of us decided to drive to Brighton for the Saturday night. The plan was that we would drive home again that night, and in the morning two of us would then catch a train to Brighton to watch the game. We had a few drinks before arriving in Brighton at about eight o'clock. We walked up West Street and noticed a small group of Millwall fans in front of us. We went into a pub and as we did so, a group of eight or so lads steamed out passed us and charged up the road towards the small group of Millwall fans that had been in front of us. Shortly afterwards, the lads returned to the pub and came straight over to us. "Fucking Millwall?" they asked.

"No way", we replied. "We don't even like football. We're just here for the night out."

Luckily, the lads appeared to believe us and decided not to give us a kicking. We casually ordered some drinks and attempted to drink them while pretending that we didn't have a care in the world. When we finished our drinks, we left the pub, politely saying "Goodnight" to the lads who had questioned us earlier.

We soon found another pub and decided to stay in there until closing time. When we left we walked towards the car, passing various groups of locals all searching for Millwall fans. At one stage there was a brief fight, but this was really handbags at six paces and was over before it had started. We left Brighton relieved that we had got away without getting a good hiding. On the way home we stopped by the side of the road for a piss and I was so drunk I fell into a stream full of sewerage.

The following morning, we woke up early and caught the train to Brighton. My companion was still feeling the effects of the drink and proceeded to be sick throughout the journey. When we got to the ground, we got chatting to some Millwall fans who told me about their night in Brighton. They said that small fights had been going on all over the town. After closing time, a lot of Millwall had gone to a night-club called The Pink Coconut where they ended up getting involved in a huge fight with some Portsmouth boys. At least one Millwall fan had been cut and spent the night in hospital.

As a result of these clashes, the Millwall fans were not a happy lot before the game, and a large mob had gathered in the park opposite the ground, awaiting the arrival of the Brighton boys. When they failed to turn up, we entered the large open side terrace and settled down to watch the game.

Millwall were clear favourites to win the game and started brightly by taking an early lead. This goal was met by a large pitch invasion by the Millwall fans. Having scored the opener though, the players seemed to think they had done enough and decided to give up. Brighton equalised and a few of their fans ran onto the pitch. They scored another and more fans ran onto the pitch. A third goal was scored and even more fans ran onto the pitch. Finally, Brighton scored their fourth and when their fans ran onto the pitch to celebrate the goal, they were met by hordes of angry Millwall fans who chased them back off their own pitch.

The season was effectively over as a result of this diabolical performance. Millwall had been so close to getting to Wembley for the first time in their history. The fans were desperate for this and were distraught to see Millwall lose in such convincing fashion. There was a slim chance that Millwall would pull the tie around at The Den, but I was so pissed off I did not even bother going to the game.

I was not quite so excited about the prospect of the 1991/92 season. The manner of the defeat at Brighton in the play-off game had really pissed me off and the inevitable departure of Sherringham to Nottingham Forest had not exactly helped either. Although he was never my favourite player, it was almost entirely down to his prolific strike rate that Millwall got into a position to challenge for promotion. He could and maybe should have left the club at the end of 1989/90, but he chose to stay for one more year. Even now, from time to time, you still see Teddy at the odd Millwall game and he always gets a good reception from the crowd.

The money raised from the sale of Teddy was not fully invested in a replacement, and many of us wondered where the goals were going to come from. We still had a good team and on occasions looked like we could challenge for promotion, but a lot of the time we threw away points, particularly away from home, and reading between the lines, you sensed that a few players were not happy with the strict Rioch regime. A lot of the players appeared to not want to battle for the team, and the fans were slowly, but surely beginning to turn on Bruce Rioch. At the same time, Reg Burr was planning on selling our beloved Den and moving the club to a new purpose built stadium at Senegal Fields, half a mile away.

Fans of all clubs love their own stadium, no matter how bad the ground may be, and Millwall fans were certainly no different. Nearly every fan opposed the proposed move. Burr was correct in saying The Den was unsuitable for top flight football, but did he really expect to see Millwall play in the top flight again? Certainly, most of the fans did not, and despite countless promises to the contrary, players were sold to finance the move. Without these players, it was going to be impossible to gain promotion and therefore it seemed pointless building a stadium ready for the big time while at the same time selling the very players who were capable of getting the club promoted. The club had been mismanaged for years and it seemed highly unlikely that a clown like Burr would be able to keep to the strict budget he had promised. 1991/92 was not a happy season for Lions fans.

The draw for the Third Round of the FA Cup paired us with Huddersfield at Leeds Road. Millwall beat them 4-0, and briefly the fans pictured a day out at Wembley the following May. Our hopes were soon dashed as we went down at Norwich in the next round in front of 4,000 travelling fans. The Cup defeat signalled a down turn in our league form too and our league position suffered accordingly. By now, the fans were beginning to vent their anger at the manager and chants of "Rioch out!" were heard all over The Den at most home games.

In March we faced Portsmouth at Fratton Park in a game we really had to win. I travelled to the game and decided to get off the train at Havant, ready for opening time. The barmaid was not too happy with the two of us banging on the door dead on eleven o'clock. Judging by the state of her, she had only just woken up, and she certainly didn't look the most attractive barmaid in the world. After selecting Chas and Dave on the jukebox, we played pool, whilst downing pint after pint of Stella as if it was going out of fashion. It was one of those sessions where the beer flowed freely and after a couple of hours we both fell in love with the barmaid.

Whether she had sorted herself out or we were just pissed I don't know, but the thought of getting in her knickers appealed to us more than watching Millwall. Both of us were giving her the patter, but eventually we realised that we were getting nowhere and decided to give the football a chance. By now, it was already three o'clock and so we resigned ourselves to missing most of the first half. By the time we got to Fratton, Millwall were 2-0 down and it seemed pointless paying to watch the game. Unfortunately, we chose to pay up anyway, and entered the turnstiles just as Portsmouth scored their third.

I went for a piss and made a bit of a mess of myself. Another few minutes were spent cleaning myself up and by the time I left the toilets for the terraces, Millwall were 4-0 down. The away end was roaring with the chant "Rioch out!" while the Portsmouth fans next to the away end were constantly taking the piss out of us, and I soon found myself involved in an incoherent slanging match with one of their fans. A policewoman threatened to arrest me for being drunk and disorderly, and so this was the signal to leave the ground voluntarily, find a local pub, and drink more Stella.

About ten of us left at the same time and headed towards the Milton Arms. I knew this was a pub frequently used by the 6:57 crew, and the possibility of trouble soon sobered me up. I was surprised to see the pub was empty, but the reason why soon became obvious. The game was still in the first half. We carried on drinking, playing pool and keeping an eye on the scores on the TV. None of us was surprised to see Portsmouth win the game by six goals to one. The Portsmouth fans slowly started returning to the pub after the final whistle and they were not too happy so see a mob of Millwall drinking in their pub. Most of the Portsmouth fans left after seeing our little mob in there. I fully expected them to firm up in another pub and come back to have a go at us, but fortunately nothing materialised. We stayed in the pub for another hour or so and eventually left and found another pub, nearer to the station.

After a few more pints in that pub, we boarded a train and returned home. We had a few more pints in one of the pubs in the town before going for a chicken vindaloo at closing time. Whilst waiting for our dinner to arrive, my friend went to the toilet to be sick and I fell asleep at the table. After finally eating our dinner, we took a cab home and sat talking absolute bollocks to the driver.

The football had been terrible, although in truth I had not seen any of it as I was just too pissed all day to take any notice. For that reason, it had been a great day incorporating all things that are good in life; beer, football and curry. The day proved to be even more memorable as it turned out to be Bruce Rioch's last game in charge. Mick McCarthy took over the manager's role, and straight away the players started to perform better. So the season ended on a bright note. We had some good players, and now that they appeared to be happy playing for the new manager, the chances of success the following season looked a little rosier.

CHAPTER 6

1992/93 promised to be a season that would never be forgotten. It was to be the final season at The Den and the fans were hoping to leave the old ground with a bang by going up.

We started the league season promisingly and were not too downhearted when we were drawn against Arsenal in the League Cup. The match was to be played over two legs with the first game at Highbury. Millwall performed bravely and were unlucky not to leave Highbury with a 1-0 victory, but Arsenal had managed to sneak a late equaliser to set up a potential classic at The Den.

The game at Highbury was marred by a very mysterious incident. Ian Wright was playing for Arsenal that night, and being an ex-Crystal Palace player he was taking a fair bit of stick from the away end. Arsenal were awarded a throw-in in front of the Millwall fans, Wright came over to take it, and as he was preparing to do so, he suddenly dived to the floor as if he had been hit by an Inter City express train. The police and stewards were as surprised as the Millwall fans, but after rolling around on the floor like a dying man, Wright eventually got up, clutching his head. He was claiming to have been hit by a missile (a scud missile perhaps, judging by his reaction) that had been thrown from the away end.

The police launched a search for the alleged missile, but incredibly nothing was found. Judging by the reaction of Ian Wright, you would have expected to see a huge gash on his head. The TV cameras later showed no such wound. And for days after the game, the police studied close circuit TV footage of the away end, but failed to see any Millwall supporter throwing anything at Ian Wright. This was not good enough for *The Sun* however, and in the interests of national security they launched a nationwide search for "the bobble-hatted yob". They alleged that the offender had been spotted and needed to be caught to ensure the survival of the game.

All this left a nasty taste in the mouth, and much trouble was expected at the return game at The Den. The atmosphere was very hostile, and Ian Wright was booed relentlessly by the home fans. Wright had a terrible game and this appeared to have an effect on the rest of the Arsenal team. Matters were not helped when Nigel Winterburn was grounded by a genuine coin in front of the Halfway. Despite continued pressure, Arsenal did not back down though, and held out for a penalty shoot out. Needless to say, Arsenal beat us on penalties.

In November, we faced West Ham at The Den. The police were taking no chances and moved the game to the Sunday morning. Millwall beat the Irons 2-1, but the atmosphere was remarkably mute.

In January, 1993, we faced Southend at Roots Hall in the Third Round of the FA Cup. The game was postponed and eventually played during the week. The police had failed to make the game all ticket, and this decision back-fired on them when Millwall fans turned up in large numbers. The away end was soon full to capacity, leaving Millwall fans with no alternative but to watch the game from the home end. Most Millwall fans dislike Southend because they are an Essex club and have close ties with West Ham. The atmosphere was always going to be hostile, but with so many Millwall fans all over the ground, trouble was now inevitable.

Southend had a fairly useful striker playing for them that night. His name was Stan Collymore. He had an arrogant air about him and his general style of play was enough to wind up the Millwall fans. He was also an ex-Crystal Palace player, and throughout the game Collymore was naturally enough abused by the away fans. The abuse became so bad that the police decided to make arrests. Without thinking of the consequences, a 16 man snatch squad was dispatched into the away end to arrest one fan. They were met by Millwall fans and a vicious fight erupted between the police and the fans. Trouble spilled over onto the pitch and seats were ripped out and used as weapons. Seven police officers were injured. Once again, Millwall had been knocked out of the FA Cup in controversial fashion.

The season soon died a death and any chance of promotion collapsed. The final game at The Den was against Bristol Rovers. Although there was nothing riding on the game, it was a sell out. All the pubs around The Den were packed to the rafters with fans reminiscing about classic games at The Den. The atmosphere was quite relaxed, but everyone knew that there would be a series of pitch invasions throughout the game, and depending on the reaction of the police, this could lead to serious disorder.

Millwall lost the game 3-0, but the atmosphere was fantastic. There had been a few minor pitch invasions throughout the game, but shortly before the final whistle, thousands of fans flooded onto the pitch. The players and officials raced to the tunnel, but quite a few Millwall players were caught. They were stripped of their kit by fans keen to get souvenirs of the final day. The Rovers fans were very nervous as thousands of Millwall fans started ripping up the pitch and smashing up the goal posts. The police kept an eye on events, but were obviously wary of inciting trouble. After a while, the fans started to turn their attention to the directors who had been responsible for the murder of The Den. The directors box was surrounded by police and they had to stand there and take it, as lumps of turf and ripped up seats flew through the air and into the stand.

The police formed a line across the width of the pitch and slowly started to force Millwall supporters out of The Den for the final time. The police were met by a barrage of missiles and I expected to see the police baton charging the fans out of the ground. The police were remarkably patient though, and failed to retaliate. As I left the ground for the final time, I turned round to have one final look at the ground. The sight of the police being attacked by Millwall fans may be seen by many people as an appropriate final vision of The Den, but I will always remember The Den for other reasons.

It was a shit hole and was hated by visiting teams and their supporters. For this reason, it was loved by the home fans and became notorious for the intimidating atmosphere. The ground was closed down because of the behaviour of the home fans more times than any other ground in the country. The atmosphere and reputation of the crowd seemed to give the home team a goal start and it really comes as no surprise to think that Millwall held a record for years for going unbeaten at The Den. The Den 1910-1993. Gone, but certainly not forgotten.

The New Den was opened by the late John Smith, the then leader of the Labour Party, with a friendly against Portuguese giants, Sporting Lisbon. The match had been eagerly anticipated by all Lions fans since it was announced and would be everybody's first chance to sample the delights of our new home.

I caught the train to South Bermondsey and headed straight to Tropics, not far from the station. Over the last year or so, some of the lads in the Windsor had mentioned that this would probably be the pub they would use on matchdays. It was packed with the usual faces and after a few pints I decided to try some of the other pubs in the vicinity.

After my pre-match drink, I walked along Ilderton Road towards the New Den. I have to say from outside it does look a spectacular stadium, even more so than the real Den. I was disappointed to see no Millwall flags or signs on the stadium itself though. There was a large sign saying "Welcome to the New London Stadium". What was all that about? This is not supposed to be a stadium for London, it is supposed to be the new home of Millwall Football Club and its loyal fans. It appeared to most people that Reg Burr was trying to distance Millwall and its violent reputation from The New Den. This may appeal to the corporate bodies who use the stadium once in a blue moon, but it did little for the Millwall fans who had seen their beloved home taken from them and were now expected to watch second-rate footballers play in this new plastic ground every other week.

Despite their reservations, the fans turned up in numbers and were met by stewards, police, and club officials who had no idea how anything worked. Tickets had to be purchased from the ticket office in the Main Stand before you could enter the ground. The queue for the tickets took forever as no one knew where they were going to sit and none of the staff were capable of helping. Once you purchased your ticket, you then had to queue to get in to your designated seat. All this came as a bit of a shock to the people who had stood on the same spot at The Den year upon year.

I obtained a ticket for the North Stand, the away end. The concourse under the stand was drab and dreary and resembled a multi-storey car park. There were refreshment stalls, but it soon became apparent that the staff on duty could not cope with a large crowd. After a long queue, I bought a pint of piss poor warm Harp lager served in a dirty plastic pint glass. It was Reg Burr's plan that Millwall fans would arrive at the ground hours before kick-off and drink and socialise in these surroundings, rather than spend their hard earned money in one of the local pubs. Did this man live in cloud cuckoo land? Did he really believe Millwall fans were so stupid that they would put up his with endless lies and sit back and do exactly what he told us? To this day, I never drink in the ground and I certainly never eat there. We were promised top quality food from well established High Street names such as McDonalds and Pizza Hut. We were told we would be able to drink good quality lager in hospitable and comfortable surroundings. Six years on and three chairmans later, and conditions have hardly improved, and fans still drink in pubs while Millwall continue to make little or no money from the stadium.

My mood got better as the game kicked off though. The ground was nearly sold out and the noise generated by the home crowd was incredible. If it could be like this every week, then maybe, just maybe, I could grow to love the ground in the same way I loved the real Den. However, I suspected that once the initial euphoria had died down, the average home crowd would not be enough to fill the ground, and consequently the atmosphere would suffer.

I still had to wait two weeks for the first league game at the new ground. It came as no surprise to anybody that the first game of the 1993/94 season would be away, this time at Stoke. Due to financial commitments, I did not go to Stoke, but as I understand it, there was a fair bit of trouble up there that day. I don't know exactly what happened, but I do know that Stoke and Millwall fans have hated each other ever since that game, and this hatred has resulted in various clashes between the two sets of fans since.

The first home game was against Southend and was played on a Sunday afternoon as it was to be shown live on TV. As expected, the atmosphere was hardly intimidating, Millwall failed to perform on the big stage, and Southend easily won 4-1. A sure sign of things to come.

Early in the season, we faced our local rivals Charlton at the newly refurbished Valley. Charlton like to consider themselves as a friendly, well run football club who cater really well for the local community. In many ways this is true, and they are certainly the complete opposite of Millwall Football Club in this respect. Although I wish that Millwall could be run as well as Charlton, I would hate to have the same kind of support at Millwall as what you get at Charlton. Their fans appear to come from a different social background to most Millwall fans, even though their primary fan base is also South East London and North Kent. Their fans tend to view Millwall as their most hated rivals and consider most Millwall fans to be Neanderthal thugs, an opinion that most Millwall fans laugh at. On the other hand, Millwall fans treat Charlton fans with contempt and laugh at their lack of passion, their boring lifestyles, and their failure to make the short trek to The Den to watch their own team play in their big derby match. One year, I recall Charlton taking some 8,000 fans to Old Trafford for a big Cup game, but the following week not even 1,500 bothered to turn up at The Den. Gillingham regularly bring more fans to The Den for Division Two games and even Auto Windscreen Cup games than Charlton ever brought to Millwall for Division One games.

With this being the first time that Millwall had played at the Valley for a number of years, most Millwall fans were looking forward to taking over the Valley once again. It was a bit disappointing then to be allocated only 900 tickets. I had failed to secure a ticket, but decided to take my chances with a tout. As I left Charlton station, I noticed a pub just down the hill. The door was wide open and you could quite clearly see that the pub was full of Millwall fans. I thought this may be a good place to try to find a ticket. What I did not realise was that there was a stool holding the door open. As I strutted through the door, I tripped over it and went flying into the crowd. In an effort to minimise the domino effect of falling bodies, I grabbed hold of one bloke by the Stone Island badge on his jumper and tried to keep on my feet. This didn't really help matters, and had the effect of bringing him down with me and probably ruining his £180 jumper. The sound of smashing glass could be heard as, one after another, people were knocking in to each other. "What the fucking hell is going on?", a few boys shouted from the bar.

I managed to pick myself up and darted out of the pub, muttering something to my mate about it being a shit pub and that there was a better one round the corner. Luckily, there was indeed another pub just round the corner and as it turned out this was also full with Millwall. I knew some of the lads in this pub, but unfortunately none of them had a spare ticket. They were saying that some of them had tickets for the directors box. I decided to stay in the pub and carry on drinking as the chances of getting a ticket appeared to be slim. I spent the rest of the day drinking in London, and the following morning it came as no surprise to read reports of trouble in the ground. Apparently, there had been incidents in three stands, ten arrests had been made, and there had even been trouble in the directors box. It really would not have taken a lot of thought from Charlton officials to prevent this trouble - all they had to do was give Millwall a fair allocation of tickets.

In December we faced Stoke at home. It was due to be played on the final Saturday before Christmas, so Millwall moved the game to the Sunday morning so that fans could go Christmas shopping. Stoke turned up mob handed, smashing up two pubs, including Tropics, before the game. This infuriated the Millwall fans and is something that has never been forgotten by any of us. A short while later, Stoke played Charlton at the Valley, in a mid week League Cup game. As their fans left the ground, they were attacked by a mob of Millwall that had gone over there to get some revenge.

On New Year's Day, we faced Crystal Palace at the new Den. This was their first visit to the new Den and I think most of their fans wanted to get it out of the way so that they could say that they had been to our new stadium and would not need to come again. They were to be disappointed though as Millwall, inspired by Ettiene Verveer, trounced the Eagles 3-0 in a memorable performance. For many Palace fans, they were now able to boast that they had been to the new Den, but very few of them have made the short journey for games played between the two sides since.

The following week, we faced Arsenal yet again, in the Third Round of the FA Cup. Sky moved the game to a Monday night, but this did not affect the paying fans as a full house turned up. The atmosphere was just as hostile as it had been at the old Den and the stick some of the Arsenal players got was very impressive. Millwall performed well, in particular a young Ben Thatcher who marked Ian Wright out of the game. It looked like a replay at Highbury was on the cards until Arsenal snatched a late and controversial winner.

There had been a number of small, violent incidents around the ground before the game. After the game, a firm of Arsenal went to the Blind Beggar at Whitechapel to have a celebratory drink. Shortly after arriving, they noticed a mob of Millwall coming up from the tube station who appeared quite eager to join them. After a violent confrontation, Millwall were forced back onto the underground where the police ensured that they returned south of the river.

The season continued with Millwall looking a good bet for promotion. In March, we faced our old rivals, Portsmouth, at Fratton Park. This game has a history of crowd trouble and both sets of fans have been banned from each other's ground at various times. In the mid-Eighties, when Millwall were banned from Fratton Park, a number of fans were arrested on their way to the ground for being in possession of firearms. Another mob of Millwall were unable to leave the train and were forced to return to London. They got off the train at Haslemere and got themselves involved in a large fight with local youths.

There have also been countless incidents at Waterloo over the years when Portsmouth were travelling through London on their way to games. More recently, Portsmouth had brought a huge mob to Millwall the previous season for their last ever appearance at The Den, but despite having the numbers that day, they still failed to get a result.

For this game, Millwall took a large mob into Portsmouth and were drinking in a pub called The Navigator in the city centre. The 6:57 crew were also drinking in the vicinity and as soon as they heard Millwall were in The Navigator, they firmed up and attacked the pub. They had underestimated the numbers Millwall had inside though, and the fact that they included some of Millwall's top boys. They took a good hiding before making a hasty retreat. The fighting continued throughout the afternoon, but Millwall managed to stick together all day and certainly achieved a comprehensive victory over their old rivals.

Our next big game was against Nottingham Forest at the Den. Once again, the game was shown live on TV, and as such, it was moved to the Sunday afternoon. A pleasant Sunday lunchtime was spent in the Windsor, watching the stripper getting her kit off, but we managed to pull ourselves away in time for kick-off (well, almost). Forest were running away with the league that season and brought a good away support with them. Early in the first half, the Forest contingent was increased by the arrival of about 50 boys who took their position in the lower tier of the away end, closest to the East Stand. These boys looked like they had enjoyed a good drink before the game because they were ever so lively, continually abusing the Millwall fans in the East Lower.

The game itself was a cracker and with our old enemy Stan Collymore playing for Forest, the atmosphere was especially abusive. Collymore was taking a lot of stick from the home fans and as is often the case in these situations, he went on to score a goal. His celebrations involved running over to the South Stand and making obscene gestures to the young children sat at the front of the stand, and this outrageous behaviour prompted one Millwall fan to run onto the pitch in an effort to confront him. Fortunately, he was prevented from reaching Stan the man by the police.

At the other end of the ground, the tension between the 50 Forest boys in the lower tier of the away end and the hundreds of Millwall in the lower tier of the East was about to erupt. One Forest boy was especially annoying. He was noticeable because of his ridiculous hair style and his pink Stone Island jumper. He may have had too much beer before the game because he was also acting like a complete fool. At one stage a few of their boys tried to get on the pitch, but this show of bravado was quickly matched from the East lower as hundreds surged towards the corner closest to the Forest fans. To be fair, the Forest fans were quite game, but as expected the intended battle was prevented by the police.

The game ended 2-2 and hundreds of Millwall fans made their way to Surrey Docks to await the arrival of the Forest boys. A violent confrontation took place and although Forest were good, they were not good enough to cope with the amount of Millwall fans waiting for them. One of their fans took a hell of a beating. I had not seen what had actually happened to him, but I did see the end result, as did the residents of the flats overlooking the incident who were laughing and cheering on the Millwall fans as they left the scene of the crime.

Millwall failed to gain automatic promotion and so they faced the play-offs once again. This time we faced Derby, with the first leg away from home. I had visited the Baseball Ground a few weeks earlier in the league game and had enjoyed a good day out, drinking in the town centre with no trouble. It was so friendly, we even got a lift to the ground from some Derby fans we had met in the pub. Unfortunately, I could not get a ticket for the play-off game and decided not to risk travelling without a ticket on this occasion.

Millwall lost a bad tempered game 2-0 and the away fans were subjected to some harsh treatment from the Derby fans inside the ground. At the end of the game, the Derby players performed a lap of honour. They obviously believed they had done enough to win the match and only needed to turn up at The Den to complete the formalities.

The mood in the pubs before the return leg was one of anticipation. It was a huge game with a lot riding on it - a first ever appearance at Wembley and a possible place in the Premier League. It was a huge task, with Millwall needing to score at least three goals against a very good team. Most fans did not think this was likely, but with an early goal and a passionate crowd behind them, anything was possible. The worst possible scenario would be to concede an early goal.

I had booked my usual seat in the lower East, but was not surprised to see this part of the ground packed shortly after kick-off. It seemed that most people wanted to be in the seats nearest to the away end. The police were not checking the tickets and the stewards may as well not have been there for all the use they were. The mood was turning angrier by the minute with hundreds of fans stood in the aisles with no seats left. Instead of trying to resolve the seating problems, the police were more interested in threatening to arrest everyone for standing up. Obviously, one thing they are not taught during their intensive training period at Hendon is that you cannot sit in a seat which does not exist. A lot of the boys in this part of the ground had already been involved in a violent disturbance with members of the Derby Lunatic Fringe in Rotherhithe just before the game and were still buzzing with the adrenalin from that incident.

Matters came to a head when Derby scored an early goal which effectively ended our season there and then. This goal, and the aggressive and hopeless policing, was the final straw for many of us in the East lower and the police at the front of the stand were attacked. A few Millwall fans managed to get onto the side of the pitch, and seeing this, the referee had no alternative but to ask the players to leave the pitch. By any standards though, the pitch invasion itself was quite small - only a handful of fans had encroached onto the playing area and this was partly due to the severe overcrowding in this part of the stand, which was a direct result of useless policing.

Whilst the game was held up, messages were coming over the tannoy to the Millwall fans in the East lower. We were advised to walk along the side of the pitch and over to the West Stand where there were enough seats to accommodate us. This made perfect sense to the fans who tried to do as they were told. Unfortunately, the police had not heard (or could not understand) the message and continued to attack any fan who tried to get over the wall. Eventually, they relented and let us walk behind the goal and over into the West Stand. As we walked behind the goal, below the Derby fans, coins and other missiles were thrown at us by sections of the Derby support.

Most of the spare seats in the West Stand were in the upper tier, but the fans from the East found themselves in the lower tier experiencing similar problems as before. After a while though, the crowd calmed down and the players reappeared. Whether the trouble had affected the Millwall players I do not know, but they were a complete embarrassment that night and Derby raced to a 4-0 lead. This was too much for some of the fans now seated in the West Stand to stomach, and for the second time that evening a number of fans raced onto the pitch. This invasion was more serious than the earlier one, and players from both teams ran for the safety of the tunnel as about 40 Millwall fans invaded the pitch. The Derby goalkeeper, Martin Thomas, had to face one fan before he could reach safety. As the fan threw a punch at Thomas, the big Derby keeper pushed the yob to the ground, and being fitter and stronger

74

than his attacker (and it has to be said, a lot better looking too), he managed to escape before the yob could pick himself up and finish what he had started.

The police made no attempt to arrest most of the fans on the pitch that night. I assumed they would use video evidence and arrest the culprits a few days later, but as far as I know, no one, not even the lad who attacked the goalkeeper, was arrested. Outside the ground, the police were determined to prevent any further trouble, but a small mob of Millwall were hell bent on causing more grief. The Derby fans were kept inside the ground for over an hour while the police and Millwall fans clashed in the streets outside. Some Derby fans who had driven to the match were not allowed to return to their transport home, and had to come back to London the following day to pick their cars up.

It had been a sorry ending to what had been a good season. The trouble had been quite serious, but no more so than other incidents that had recently taken place. The press seemed to over react due to the fact that a player had been assaulted and two other players had been racially abused. I will look into the media coverage of this and other incidents later in this book, but for the time being it is suffice to say that sensationalising the violence that night only added to Millwall's reputation.

CHAPTER 7

An air of disillusionment hung over The Den prior to the start of the 1994/95 season. As usual Millwall had come close to achieving some sort of success, but had failed miserably at the final hurdle. This failure had been accompanied by the usual sorry scenes of violence which had been widely reported and exaggerated by the media.

Sponsors did not want to be associated with a club who only received media coverage when the fans misbehaved, and chose to keep their much needed money to themselves. This left Millwall with a large and expensive stadium which was redundant 90% of the time, and even on match days the gate receipts were not enough to pay the running costs. The promises of spectacular non-football events, such as pop concerts and world championship boxing matches, failed to materialise, and the fans were seriously concerned about the club's inability to manage its own finances.

One by one, promising young players that had come through the youth system, or had been purchased on the cheap by Bruce Rioch, were sold and replaced by either crap young players from the likes of non-league Sittingbourne or old hasbeens such as Clive Allen. Invariably, Mick McCarthy awarded these players long and lucrative contracts. The older players seemed happy to see out the end of their prosperous careers at Millwall, and took little or no interest in their own performance or the performance of the team. The younger players appeared to think they were something special now that they were fully fledged professionals, and strolled around like big time charlies.

The most annoying thing about this situation was the non-stop lies dished out by the directors at the time. When other teams made bids for certain players, the directors would announce that we were a highly ambitious club and did not need to sell our best players. A few months later, when the annual accounts were being prepared, it became obvious that Millwall had no alternative but to sell these players and sell them quick. Vultures like Crystal Palace and Wimbledon would then offer ludicrous prices for top quality players and Millwall would have no alternative but to sell.

The first game of the season was at home to Southend. I was so uninspired by the prospect of this game that I decided to stay in the pub rather than walk up the road to the ground. Despite my apathy, I still made arrangements to go to Sunderland the following week with my mate. This decision was probably taken late on Saturday night after drinking all day, but despite this, the trip went ahead as planned.

I could not afford the price of the train ticket and was a little concerned that my W reg Ford Fiesta 95Occ would not cope with the long journey. As a compromise, we decided to drive to York on the Friday afternoon where we could have a night on the piss before continuing with the journey on Saturday morning. We arrived in York at five o'clock and went drinking until two o'clock in the early hours. It had been a very enjoyable night, and I still felt pissed as I drove up the A1 to Sunderland. A large breakfast in a Little Chef failed to clear my head and by the time I arrived in Sunderland at about 2:00pm, the hangover had set in.

We had arranged to meet some other Millwall fans in The Blue Bell, near Seaburn station. I had reservations about this as I had heard that a few of the Seaburn Casuals frequented this pub on match days. The last thing I needed was another beer or a good kicking, so we decided against this and instead made our way to the ground. Unusually, the weather in Sunderland was fairly pleasant and we settled down to watch a 1-1 draw. The game was memorable for two reasons only. Kasey Keller was relentlessly booed throughout the game by the Rokerites who had not forgotten his part in the sending off of Don Johnson at the previous encounter at The Den. And our former striker, Malcolm Allen, watched the game with the Millwall fans. He was soon spotted by the Mackems, and because he was playing for Newcastle United at the time, he also took a lot of stick from the locals.

The two of us left the ground a few minutes before the end to make our way back to the car before the traffic got too bad. I was walking about ten yards behind my mate and noticed two young casuals walking towards him. As they passed him, they turned and threw a punch from behind which connected with his head. The punch was pathetic and when my friend turned round, the two lads backed off. The two of us pursued our attackers round the corner where we were confronted by a mob of seven or eight lads. One of them lunged at me with a knife, narrowly missing my face. Hopelessly outnumbered, we had no alternative but to run. Unfortunately, I went one way and my friend went the other, leaving the mob of Mackems in between us. I felt I had to get back to my

77

mate and decided to charge through the Mackems in the hope of reaching him. This must have surprised them as although I took a few kicks, I managed to reach my mate without too much trouble.

We decided to go back to the away end to see if we could get a few other Millwall to join us in having a go back at the Mackems. Millwall did not have a firm up there that day and although there were small groups of casuals, it seemed unfair to bring them into our fight so our plans for revenge came to nothing.

The police were obviously aware that something had happened though and pulled the two of us over for questioning. We told them our story, and judging by their reaction they obviously knew who the attackers were. They asked us to get in their car and drive around with them in the hope that we could identify them. There was no way we were going to grass these people up - if we wanted revenge we could always get it at the return game at The Den.

The police were disappointed at our refusal to help them with their enquiries and this left us with a bit of a problem. We wanted their help in getting to our car in safety, but as we had refused to help them they were going to refuse to help us. Luckily for us, the driver of one of the police dog vans was an exiled Londoner and despite the fact that he was a West Ham fan, he agreed to give us a lift to our car.

When we reached the car, he was dismayed to see a Capital Radio sticker on the back window. The traffic was at a stand still and if some of the locals spotted the sticker on the car we could be in danger. He decided there was no alternative but to give my car a police escort out of Sunderland. Obviously, he hadn't thought about simply removing the sticker from the window, but his idea sounded quite exciting and so I kept quiet. We followed the police van, sirens blaring, all the way to the A1 whilst the natives tried to peer in the windows to see which member of the royal family was driving the orange Fiesta through Sunderland. The car made it all the way home, although at one stage we were overtaken by a Robin Reliant. A few months later, the car blew up returning home from a game at Port Vale.

Our next home game was against Derby County who had failed to gain promotion despite beating us in the play-offs last season. Many of us thought Derby would bring a huge mob to Millwall to seek revenge for what had happened at the previous game, but as it turned out, they brought hardly any fans with them and the players certainly were not happy about returning to the Den so soon after the last encounter. Millwall ran out convincing winners, 4-1.

The draw for the League Cup paired us with Mansfield at Field Mill. This was a new ground for most of the Millwall fans and a fair few people decided to make the journey up the M1 on the Wednesday night. Bearing in mind the close proximity of Mansfield to both Derby and Nottingham, two teams with good reason to dislike Millwall, I thought that there might be some trouble at the game. We parked in one of the large superstore car parks near to the ground and walked through an alley to the match. I was very wary as it was obvious Mansfield had a large mob out and about who were clearly looking for Millwall fans. Luckily, they did not click who we were and we managed to get safely into the ground to witness a good away win. I later heard that a mob of Millwall had earlier been involved in clashes with Mansfield fans in a town centre pub. This may explain why such a large and intimidating mob was waiting near the ground on our way in.

In the next round, we were paired with Nottingham Forest at the City Ground. The potential for violence at this game was quite high in view of the severity of the fighting at The Den the previous season. We drove to the game and parked in a pub car park not far from the ground. It was about five o'clock and the pub was fairly quiet. Upon hearing our accents, the barman deduced that we were Millwall fans and continued to make a series of witty remarks about how the three of us were going to smash his pub up, nick his money, and rape all of his female customers. We did not bite and tried to convince him that not all Millwall fans were as bad as the press had made out. We were smartly dressed, quiet, and polite, and he was just about to come around to our way of thinking, when one of his barmaids came into the pub. She looked like she had just seen a ghost and could hardly get her words out.

Eventually, she stopped shaking and started telling how she had been near a pub called the Royal Children in the town centre which had been smashed up by hordes of drunken Millwall fans. This was enough to convince the locals that we were bullshitting and so we decided to drink up and go to the ground to find out what had really happened.

It transpired that about 60 Millwall boys had hired a coach and had found themselves drinking in the Royal Children for two hours in the afternoon. A mob of Forest approached the pub, but were prevented from getting too close by a large police presence. Millwall tried to leave the pub to get at Forest, but were also prevented from doing so by the police. While all this was going on, considerable damage was caused to the pub. After the Forest fans had been dispersed, the police entered the pub where they found eight knives that had been dropped on the floor. The police did not make any arrests, but would not let the Millwall fans leave the pub unless they contributed to the cost of the repairs. Every one of the Millwall fans had to hand over a fiver to the police that night before they were taken to the ground. I dare say the police passed this £300 onto the brewery or the insurance company, but wouldn't it be nice to think that they pocketed the money themselves and put it towards a jolly up.

Millwall had about 1,500 fans at the game that night and most of them were casual lads who were well up for it. Nearly all of them were sat nearest to the Executive Stand as this is where the Forest boys, the Forest Executive Crew (FEC), used to sit. They were disappointed to see only a handful of Forest boys in the stand, but one familiar face did stick out. The idiot with the silly haircut and the pink Stone Island jumper was in the lower tier with a few of his cronies. This time he was not so mouthy, maybe because he was not as drunk as before or maybe because he was only with a few mates. Either way, the Millwall boys relentlessly took the piss out of his flowing blonde locks throughout the game, and with about ten minutes to go he left the ground looking completely humiliated. To add to his misery, Millwall had beaten Forest and now faced Swindon in the Quarter Finals.

A few weeks earlier we had stuffed Swindon at the County Ground so expectations were high that we would beat them and get into the Semi Finals. The dream was of a Wembley Cup Final and a place in Europe. Now, that would be interesting.

I travelled to Swindon without a ticket, but managed to buy one from a tout on the train. As usual, most of the pubs in Swindon were closed, but we did manage to find one about 15 minutes walk from the town centre. The pub was packed full of Millwall eagerly looking forward to the big game, but once again we were all to be disappointed. Millwall conceded three goals before they managed to snatch a late consolation goal. A 3-1 defeat at Swindon was a terrible way to go out of the Cup after such high expectations, and I felt thoroughly miserable as I left the ground. Apart from a few minor incidents in the stand to our left and outside by the park, there had been no major trouble.

This defeat left us with just the league and the FA Cup to concentrate on, and yet again we were paired with Arsenal in the Cup. This was becoming very frustrating because although we always played well against them we could never get a result. The game at The Den was just like all the others, with Millwall outplaying Arsenal, but failing to score. We did manage to get a replay so at least we had a second opportunity to progress.

Fortunately for us, Arsenal were going through the George Graham bung scandal at the time and the players were not performing to their usual high standards. As they ran onto the Highbury pitch, morale must have been at an all time low. Millwall managed to take advantage of this and went one goal up early doors, courtesy of Mark Beard. It seemed inevitable that Arsenal would snatch an undeserved equaliser, but late in the second half, Mark Kennedy raced clear down the left wing and smashed the ball past David Seaman to send the Clock End into raptures. It was one of the greatest results in the history of the club, and more than made up for the disappointment of Swindon.

Things got even better when we were paired with Chelsea at the Den in the next round. The game was immediately made all ticket and I posted a request for my usual seat in the East Lower. Unfortunately, due to a postal strike, my letter was not received until all the tickets had already been sold, so this left me with no alternative but to use the services of a tout once again. Although I was charged over the odds, I was really grateful for the ticket. Touts really do provide a service to genuine fans and I would never criticise them. If you don't want to pay what they ask, you don't have to. My only regret was that the ticket was for the South Stand.

Chelsea firmed up in North Lambeth and made their way to Bermondsey. They turned up with a very impressive mob and although they were confronted by small groups of Millwall as they approached the ground, Millwall were not organised enough to do such a large mob. Inside the ground, Chelsea filled the North Stand and also had small pockets of fans in other parts of the stadium. In particular, they had a good little mob in the West Stand who were involved in violent clashes with Millwall fans throughout the game.

The game was crap and finished 0-0. Just before the end, I noticed Chelsea firming up at the bottom of the North Stand, close to the West Stand. They walked along the front of the North Stand towards the East lower, and without hesitation, steamed straight past the police and stewards and into the waiting Millwall fans. A huge fight erupted and although Millwall had the numbers, Chelsea stood their ground and gave as good as they got. Chelsea had instigated the trouble and without doubt their main boys were involved in this skirmish. I have met some of these boys at England away games and I have to say they are some of the most game blokes I have ever seen at football. More and more Millwall fans rushed to this corner of the East Stand to join in the fight yet still they failed to run Chelsea back into their end. It eventually took a dozen mounted police and countless other officers on foot a full 15 minutes to restore peace to the ground.

After the game, Chelsea were escorted to South Bermondsey train station where they were confronted by more Millwall fans. This time, quite a few Chelsea managed to escape from the escort and chased these Millwall fans away. The Chelsea mob headed into the estates, looking for Millwall, and attacked three pubs, including the Braincote Arms, before the police managed to regain control of the situation.

The replay was always going to be a troublesome encounter, but as it turned out, the way the game went meant it was particularly violent. We left Fulham Broadway station to be met by a thick line of police, horses and dogs and we walked the short distance to the ground accompanied all the way by the police. There was a heavy atmosphere and everywhere you looked there were mobs of casual lads waiting on the streets for something to happen. They were not dishing out threats like you get at other grounds because they did not need to. Likewise, the Millwall fans were not singing or shouting or giving it the big one. Everyone, including the police, knew something big was going to happen. It was just a question of when.

I took up my position in the lower tier of the East Stand and was pleased to see that Millwall had also been allocated the temporary South Stand. All in all, there were about 6,000 Millwall fans in the ground and nearly all of them were young men in their twenties and thirties. A brief look around the ground indicated that the Chelsea support was primarily made up of similar people. It was not a night for women or children.

Millwall went 1-0 up and this was the signal for a celebratory pitch invasion by a number of Millwall fans in the East Stand. The home fans were not happy at our show of bravado, but later in the game Chelsea equalised to force the game into extra time. No further goals were scored and so it was down to the dreaded penalty shoot out. This was the worst possible scenario for the police because they knew that whoever lost would go mental.

As it turned out, Millwall won and so it was down to Chelsea to kick things off. Whilst we were celebrating another glorious victory over hated London rivals, Chelsea fans ran on the pitch from the North Stand and attacked Dave Mitchell and Ben Thatcher. The players managed to escape from the pitch and so Chelsea decided to confront the Millwall fans at the other end of the ground. They started running across the pitch towards us, but a line of police, 28 on horseback, had formed on the halfway line and managed to prevent Chelsea getting near to us. One fan did manage to get through the police line, but as he approached the 6,000 Millwall fans, he suddenly realised he was on his own. Rather sheepishly, he turned around to return to the North Stand. When he got back to the apparent safety of the North Stand, some Chelsea fans must have thought he was a Millwall fan and they gave him a good kicking. He was then pulled away by the police and arrested. I don't think he will have fond memories of this night.

As all this trouble was kicking off, Millwall had stopped celebrating and were now fighting the police at the front of the South Stand. They were determined to get onto the pitch to fight Chelsea, but the police were holding firm and managed to prevent them from doing so. Meanwhile, in the West Stand, Chelsea were also fighting the police as well as ripping the stand to pieces so that they could arm themselves ready for the clash on the pitch. When it became apparent that the 400 police on duty were not going to give in to the fans requests, Chelsea decided to throw the weapons at the police and the Millwall supporters.

We left the ground to see what was happening outside. Chelsea quickly followed and the night air was soon filled with the sound of it kicking off. Most of the Millwall turned left towards Sloane Square and when Chelsea tried to follow us, the police baton charged Chelsea back towards Fulham Broadway. Eventually, Chelsea managed to find Millwall up near Earls Court and the fighting was so severe that the police had to close Earls Court and Fulham Broadway tube stations. One fan was stabbed and 38 others were arrested.

A week after this game, England fans went on the rampage in Dublin before and during a friendly game against Ireland. The trouble inside the ground was so bad the game had to be abandoned. In the media, Chelsea and Millwall fans took a lot of the blame for this trouble, but that was completely unjustified. I went to Dublin and nearly all the trouble was caused by Northern firms. Millwall or Chelsea had no real mob over there. However, football violence was once again big news and it was reported in the media that all sorts had been planned for our next game in the Cup against QPR the following Saturday. There were reports that Chelsea fans would be at Loftus Road, seeking revenge against Millwall. Revenge for what, I asked myself? Chelsea fans had started most of the trouble at our two games and if anyone was after revenge, it would have to be Millwall.

I did not have a ticket for the match, but managed to buy one from a tout in the bookies by the Springbok pub. The ticket was for the home end, but I suspected that a few Millwall would be in with me as there were plenty of ticketless fans outside. Millwall played well, but in the last minute Damian Webber conceded a daft penalty. The police went crazy, obviously thinking this would spark off the trouble. Hundreds of police and stewards surrounded the away end as QPR prepared to take the penalty. The penalty was converted and the police were more than ready for the expected outburst of hooliganism. Nothing happened though and the Millwall supporters left West London demoralised at the sad ending of another glorious Cup run.

The season faded out with Millwall slipping alarmingly down the league. Fortunately though, we had gained enough points at the start of the season to not have any serious concerns about relegation - this time.

CHAPTER 8

In August, 1995, at the start of the 1995/96 season, Millwall faced Reading at Elm Park in a mid week match. I always find Reading a boring place to visit and this evening was no exception. We drove to Reading, had a few beers, watched a mediocre game and drove home without further incident.

I was living at home at the time and was woken up by my mother the following morning. "Were you involved in all that bother last night?"

I tried to recollect where I had been and thought about the game. I had not seen any trouble in the ground and would have been shocked if anything big had happened in the town after the game. I switched on the radio and listened to the news. "Millwall yobs attack players!" screamed the newscaster.

It turned out that a 15 year old boy had thrown a spark plug onto the pitch during the game. It landed by the touchline, nowhere near any player. A steward had seen the incident and removed the weapon from the playing area, whilst the police arrested the young culprit. What the boy did was a stupid thing, of that there is no doubt, but no real harm was done and no one was hurt. The culprit was arrested and the game was not held up. Why then was this headline news throughout the country? On the same night, there had been two shootings and 13 stabbings at the Notting Hill carnival, but this did not attract the same headlines. The spark plug was a nothing incident, but because it had been perpetrated by a Millwall supporter, the media deemed it newsworthy.

A month later we faced Everton at the Den in the League Cup. I arrived at the Barnaby for my pre-match drink and as the taxi approached the pub, I noticed a firm of boys standing around by the front door. I assumed that the pub would be busy and that these lads were Millwall who were just drinking outside. The taxi dropped us right outside the pub, right in the middle of this mob. As soon as I stepped out of the cab and had a good look at the faces, I realised they were not Millwall. They were Scousers and they were arguing with each other about whether to smash this pub up or go elsewhere. I did not want to be outside the Barnaby with the Scousers if they did attack the pub and thought it would be safer if I could join the Millwall fans inside. The Barnaby is not a boys pub, but on most match days there are a few boys who would be prepared to fight back if a mob did cause trouble.

We scurried past the Scousers and into the pub. I took one look around and saw it was not even half full. For a game like this I expected the pub to be packed, but for some reason it was virtually empty. To make matters worse, and on closer inspection, a lot of the boys in the pub were also Scousers. The mob of Scousers were still outside and I realised that if they did steam into the pub, we would be liable for a good kicking. We decided to try to leave the pub and take our chances outside.

I came out of the pub and tried to walk straight through the Scousers without being noticed. I didn't have much luck and was soon pulled over by a few of their boys. I was well aware of the reputation Scousers widely have in football for slashing fans when caught on their own. I fully expected a blade across my cheek, but to be fair to the Scousers, all they wanted to know was where our boys were drinking. I quickly pointed out that if they wanted a row they should go over to Bermondsey where there would be quite a few Millwall who would be happy to oblige them. Fortunately, they took my advice and headed off towards South Bermondsey train station, while I headed off to the Windsor in desperate need of a stiff drink.

Once I had regained my composure, I turned around and saw that the police had pulled the Scousers over just up the road from the Barnaby. Later on I heard that they had dropped a large knife just before the police could search them. My initial instincts had been correct.

This game ended in a draw and so the following week we made the return trip to Goodison fully expecting more trouble. In all honesty, the Millwall support was quite disappointing, but those who were there witnessed the Lions come back from a 2-0 deficit to win 4-2. Another glorious Cup run was on the cards.

In October we faced Crystal Palace at Selhurst and Sheffield Wednesday at the Den in the next round of the League Cup. Chubby Brown had done Millwall fans a great favour by releasing *Living Next Door To Alice; Who The Fuck Is Alice?*. It didn't take a lot to work out that Millwall fans would change the word Alice to Palace and adopt this song for the game. Millwall beat Palace 2-1 and the whole Arthur Wait stand reverberated to the chant of "Palace, Palace, who the fuck are Palace?", much to the embarrassment of ITV who failed to edit the song from the live transmission of the game.

We were easily outclassed by Sheffield Wednesday however, and they ran out 2-0 winners on the night. Once again I was woken the following morning by my mum who demanded to know if I had been involved in all the trouble Millwall fans had caused the night before. I listened to the radio and found out that one idiot had walked onto the pitch and said something to Kevin Pressman. I must admit I had not seen this incident, but by all accounts, the bloke was arrested almost straight away. He hadn't hit the goalkeeper and had caused no damage, apart from to his own reputation. The press made out that this was a terrible incident and it was headline news for days afterwards, with reports of how Kevin Pressman feared for his life, believing the yob could have been armed with a knife. The bloke who committed the crime was obviously an idiot who was not capable of causing damage to a choir boy, let alone a strapping professional athlete like Pressman.

It was completely different to the incident that happened at the Derby match. That night the goalkeeper was physically attacked by a fan, but managed to push the fan to the ground before any real damage could be caused. In fact, Martin Thomas was not even hurt, where as the fan who attacked him had to pick himself up off the floor and clean his muddy jeans in front of all his mates. Highly embarrassing! On top of all that, he then had to watch his escapade on TV for weeks after.

The Pressman incident was stupid, but it is a fact of life that situations such as this occur from time to time at grounds all over the country. It is only ever widely reported when it happens at The Den though, and this gives people who do not follow football the impression that it is a problem confined to Millwall. This could not be further from the truth.

The season was going quite well though, and in November we faced Birmingham at St Andrews in a top of the table clash. Millwall demanded that the game be made all ticket in view of its importance and the fact that there would be a large travelling support, but Karen Brady knew better, and despite pleas from the West Midlands Police, she decided that fans could pay at the turnstile on the day of the match.

I travelled on a coach to St Andrews and was dropped off in the car park behind the main stand. As I was walking to the turnstile, I saw a mob of 30 or so Blues coming towards us. They charged at us and although we were not in a firm, we had no choice but to stand our ground as we were penned up against the wall of the stand. A brief flurry of punches was thrown before the police separated the two sets of fans. I was then amazed to see the same Blues going through the turnstiles in the same stand that we were in. I was under the impression that we had been allocated the whole of the Railway Stand, but as it turned out Karen Brady had decided that we would be unable to fill the whole stand ourselves and so had decided to allocate the top tier to the home fans. Not only was this bad enough, but this part of the ground was not made all ticket and so every hooligan that had ever followed Birmingham took up his position in the seats directly above the Millwall fans.

As kick-off approached, it soon became apparent that there was not enough room in the lower tier for all the away fans and a lot of people were forced to stand in the aisles. A mob of about 80 Millwall entered the ground shortly after kick-off and were amazed to see a mass of Blues right above us.

Throughout the game, Birmingham fans threw missiles at the Millwall supporters below, and some of their fans ran onto the pitch and attacked our winger, Dave Savage, while the police and stewards stood back and watched. Golf balls, fireworks, flasks, rubbish bins, coins, and all sorts were landing on innocent fans' heads. A few days later, Karen Brady slated the Millwall fans because a home made hand grenade was found in the lower tier after the game. She obviously did not realised that it was probably in the Millwall end because it had been thrown there by her own fans.

The missiles continued until such time as the Millwall fans finally retaliated. As the game was coming to an end, Millwall started to rip up the seats and throw them at the home fans sitting directly above us. These were returned by the Blues and for a while it was like a scene from a West Belfast news flash. When the game finally finished, the Millwall supporters were kept in for over an hour while the Blues went on the rampage in the streets around the ground. The Millwall team coach and some of the supporters coaches were smashed up and a police horse was stabbed. Eventually, Millwall fans were allowed out and were escorted under heavy police escort to New Street station.

Again headlines were made, but this time the press seemed to stick up for Millwall. Only one Millwall fan had been arrested all day and that was for being drunk and disorderly (no, it wasn't me), but incredibly Karen Brady announced to anyone who cared to listen that

Millwall supporters were to blame. She completely disregarded the fact that she had put everyone at risk, including her own fans, by failing to listen to the London police, West Midlands Police and Millwall Football Club. She had chosen to put bums on seats and make a few extra pounds rather than consider the safety of the paying public. When trouble had occurred as a direct result of her incompetence, her only form of defence was to attack Millwall and its supporters by claiming we were to blame. She stated that Birmingham was a friendly family club and that the fans had never been involved in any trouble.

She clearly had forgotten the pre-season friendly against Celtic which had been marred by serious violence only a few months earlier. She has clearly never been to an England away game where she would see that the Blues have one of the most feared hooligan gangs in the country. She obviously forgot the battle Stoke and Birmingham fans played out on the pitch at St Andrews a few years earlier. She may even have forgotten the death of a young Birmingham fan who died while Leeds and Birmingham fans were fighting each other on the pitch at St Andrews in 1985. Anyone who goes to football regularly will know that Birmingham have a huge hooligan element, and to put them in the seats directly above Millwall fans in a high profile game had to be the most ludicrous decision since West Ham signed Marcus Boogers.

Did she really expect anyone to believe that Millwall supporters smashed their own coaches up and attacked one of their own players? She even went as far as saying Millwall Football Club should be banned because the fans attract trouble wherever they go. Does this mean that next time a firm attacks Birmingham fans, her precious football club should be closed down? In many ways she was very clever because she must have been all too aware that many ill-informed people would believe her lies because so many people have a preconceived idea of what Millwall supporters are like.

The Millwall officials maintained a dignified silence in sharp contrast to the hysterical rantings that came from Brady. The police agreed that the trouble had been caused by City fans, but despite this, the name of Millwall had once again been dragged through the gutter. I am the first to admit that Millwall has a hooligan element and some of the bad press we get is justified. On this occasion though, Millwall fans were not to blame and Brady should have been big enough to admit it. Mud sticks and despite the fact that Millwall were cleared by the police and the FA, many people would have seen the headlines and assumed that we were to blame. Karen Brady and her little husband, Paul Peschisolido, will never ever be forgiven by Millwall fans for the events that night.

Millwall stayed near the top of the league until Christmas, but just like the previous two years, they started to fade, this time with disastrous results. When the going got tough, McCarthy got going and buggered off to Dublin to take control of Ireland. His legacy was a crop of players on lucrative long term contracts who could be classed as some of the worst players ever seen at Millwall.

In March we faced Crystal Palace at the Den. Jimmy Nicholl had taken over at the helm, but was powerless to prevent the slide down the table. Palace hammered us 4-1 and the embarrassment of losing to Palace was too much to take for some fans. Some individuals attempted to orchestrate a pitch invasion, but their efforts were thwarted by the police, and after the game, a number of innocent Palace fans were attacked on their way to South Bermondsey train station.

In April, it was Birmingham's turn to visit the Lions' Den. It came as no surprise to anyone that Brady failed to turn up. What was more surprising though was the pathetic away support. There could not have been more than 150 Blues at the Den that night. I did hear a rumour though that a mob of Blues was prevented from travelling by the police. I don't know if this is true, but if they really wanted to come to London that night, they could easily have done so. Maybe they wanted to be stopped.

Most of the Blues turned up on official club buses and as they passed the Barnaby, the coaches were attacked by bottle throwing Millwall fans. By our standards, there was a large crowd at the game that night and it seemed that almost everyone in the East Stand was there to fight the Blues. Millwall comfortably won the game 2-0 and the atmosphere all night was incredibly hostile, and in the absence of any real away support, their players took the brunt of the abuse.

Despite winning the game, a large minority of Millwall fans left the ground with other things on their mind. It was obvious the police would not let Millwall anywhere near the Birmingham fans, and when a line of police prevented Millwall from getting at their rivals the inevitable happened. Missiles were thrown at the police who then retaliated by charging Millwall through the local estates. The running battles went on for some time and made headline news the following morning.

The following week we faced the clayheads from Stoke at home. With the Lions slipping perilously close to relegation and Stoke challenging for promotion, a large crowd turned up for a real six-pointer. Stoke beat us 3-2 in a classic match, but what made the day even more memorable was the fact that Stoke had brought a large mob to the Den. This mob was bolstered by members of the Dundee Utility Firm, although I understand some of them were prevented from reaching London so their numbers could have been even bigger. They were actually supposed to turn up in Peckham before the game, but failed to do so.

Inside the ground, the police separated their mob from the rest of their support. Most of us found it highly amusing to think that Stoke needed the help of a Scottish firm before they had the nerve to turn up at the Den. I must admit I have never been to Dundee, but it strikes me that Dundee or Dundee United can't be too clever if they have to mob up with each other in order to get a half decent firm together. I understand they do so because neither of them is capable of doing a firm from Edinburgh or Aberdeen without the help of their arch rivals. If this is true, what does it say about Stoke? All I know is that they failed to get any kind of a result that day, even with the help of their Scottish friends, and since that day they have failed to show in numbers against Millwall, either home or away.

In the final week of the season every result went against us, leaving us in serious danger of getting relegated. Our last game was at Ipswich on the Sunday. A good away following made the relatively short journey to East Anglia where we were met by hordes of riot police. The town centre had shut down for the day and most Millwall fans walked around aimlessly until kick-off.

Despite a brave performance, Millwall failed to get the victory they desperately needed. A 0-0 draw meant that we were relegated because fellow relegation candidates, Portsmouth, had achieved a result at Huddersfield. The Millwall players trudged off the pitch whilst the Ipswich fans raced out of the ground. We were left in the away end surrounded by riot police banging their truncheons against their legs. We all knew that it would kick off at some point, it just needed a spark. Suddenly, the Portsmouth result was announced over the tannoy. Gleefully, it was announced that as a result of this score, Millwall were now relegated.

It was a stupid thing to say and was enough to spark an evening of violence. Seats were ripped out and thrown at the departing Ipswich fans and the police. Outside the ground, a series of running battles ensued all the way back to the train station. When the fans arrived back in London, many of them headed towards the East End to confront old rivals, West Ham. There was more fighting at Mile End and on the tube.

The violence was disappointing, but I can't say I was surprised. To me, the most disappointing thing about the day was the crocodile tears shed by the likes of Kasey Keller and Ben Thatcher. These players were responsible for the position Millwall Football Club now found itself in, and I knew as well as they did that they would be on their way out of Millwall. I appreciate the fact that they had to do what was best for them and their families, but why go through the charade of pretending you care about the club and its supporters. To the players, the club is just an employer, a means of making money out of doing something they enjoy. To the fans, it is a huge part of life and we were the ones who had every reason to be genuinely disappointed, not them.

After the initial shock and disappointment of relegation, I began to look forward to the start of the 1996/97 season. Although a few players had deserted us in our hour of need, on paper at least the team looked strong enough to push for promotion back to Division One. Shortly before the start of the season, Jimmy Nicholl returned to Raith Rovers to purchase some players from his former club. Apparently, he knew these players well and believed they possessed the sufficient quality Millwall needed to climb out of the mess we found ourselves in. To be fair, Steve Crawford looked to have half decent credentials and had already been capped by Scotland. And Paul Hartley was a light weight winger who had an array of tricks up his sleeve. Jason "Dan" Dair was just crap. Most amusing of all though, was the new centre back, David "Sincy" Sinclair.

Nicholl was so pleased with his new recruits that he invited the media down to the Den for a photo opportunity with our new stars fitted out in full Scottish regalia of kilt and sporran. No doubt, they wore no underwear as this is the tradition amongst real Scots. Nicholl proudly declared that Sincy was so hard he had tattoos on his teeth, a feature that he assumed would make him popular with Millwall fans. If Nicholl believed that buying a player because he was hard would endear him to Millwall fans, he was sadly mistaken. The fact was that Sinclair was an absolute waste of space. The fact that he was Scottish as well as crap made him even more unpopular. Nicholl had only been at Millwall a short while, but he obviously did not have a clue what Millwall was all about. When news of our new signings was reported in the papers under the heading "McMillwall" this infuriated many fans who were already annoyed with the directors responsible for the running of the club because of the disaster of the previous season. Before the new season had even started, Nicholl and the directors were not doing well in the popularity stakes.

It had been arranged that Liverpool would play a friendly at the Den as part of the deal negotiated with them for the sale of Mark Kennedy. Liverpool finally managed to fulfil this fixture a week before the official start of the season. It had seemed like years since the Ipswich game and I could not wait for the start of another season. I was so excited in the Barnaby before this friendly match that I didn't notice how well the beers were going down. I left the pub shortly before kick-off and as I walked past a police van I felt the sudden urge to be sick. It was too late to stop myself and so I threw up all over the pavement right next to the van. As I was being sick, I fully expected one of the coppers to come out and arrest me for being drunk and disorderly. Fortunately for me, they saw the funny side and remained in the van laughing at me.

After my sudden bout of sickness, I felt much better and was pleased to see our old friend, Stan Collymore, out on the pitch with his new club. Despite the fact that the game was supposed to be a friendly, the Millwall fans abused Collymore throughout. He really is so easy to wind up and you could see him getting more and more annoyed as the game went on. Eventually, his frustration boiled over and he elbowed his marker in the head. The referee saw the incident, but instead of sending him off, he advised the Liverpool bench to substitute him. I may be mistaken, but I was under the impression that assaulting another player is a sending off offence in any match, not just Premier League games.

The first league game of the season saw Wrexham at the Den. 9,371 turned up to witness our return to Division Two, a fine crowd in the circumstances, especially when you consider the lack of away fans. The vast majority of the crowd went home disappointed though as Millwall struggled to a 1-1 draw.

The disappointment continued as Millwall failed to break down teams and were knocked out of the League Cup at Peterborough after losing on penalties. This shoot out was memorable because you could see the players arguing because none of them had the bottle to take a penalty. This was a poxy League Cup game at

Peterborough, not a World Cup Semi Final, and was a sure sign of the poor attitude most of the players had.

Things did liven up briefly with the arrival on loan of a striker from Newcastle by the name of Darren Huckerby. He scored on his debut and generally terrified opposing defenders with his speed. He was clearly a player with immense talent and the crowd loved him. He said all the right things in the media and made it clear he would rather play regular first team football with Millwall than sit idle at Newcastle who did not even have a reserve team at the time.

Nicholl made efforts to sign him, but Newcastle said they wanted one million pounds for the player. This seemed a reasonable amount for a player of his potential, but Millwall would only stretch to £750,000. A compromise could not be reached and Huckerby regrettably returned to Tyneside. A few weeks later, Coventry paid one million pounds for Huckerby and within a few months he had set the Premier League alight with his devastating turn of pace and eye for goal. His value soared to over five million and he was touted as a future England star. It was clear to all Millwall fans who saw his performances for the Lions that Millwall had a player who could have turned our fortunes around. With him in our team, we would almost certainly have been promoted that season. The club could then have sold him, making a substantial profit. I can't believe the directors were so stupid to deliberately let him go. There were obviously things they were not telling us about the real state of our finances. As usual, Millwall talked a good game, but when push came to shove, they failed to produce the goods. This was a decision they must have regretted a few months later.

In October we faced away games at Gillingham and Brentford. These games were now considered to be our big derby games, but it is quite sad when you sink to such a level that you look forward to going to Brentford. The fact that there is a pub on each corner of the ground can not disguise the fact that Brentford is a dull and boring place to visit. Gillingham is slightly better and the atmosphere at this game was quite hostile. Millwall had sold out their allocation and quite a few Millwall fans had purchased tickets for the home end, resulting in minor skirmishes on the terraces throughout the game. Millwall beat the Gills quite convincingly, and on this performance really looked like they were heading back to Division One.

In November we were drawn away to Woking in the First Round of the FA Cup. Although it was always going to be a tricky game, it was a good draw in a way because Sky had decided to show the match live on TV. Millwall were obviously in dire need of any money they could get and the TV cash would come in handy. To accommodate Sky, the game was moved to the Friday night.

The game ended 2-2, but I was so pissed and so cold that I did not really care what the final score was. As we left the ground, a number of locals threw some coins at us, but with Millwall having quite a good little firm there that night, the Woking boys didn't really want to know. There were a few skirmishes near the ground and also in one of the pubs near the station, but nothing too bad.

Sky also televised the replay at the Den and although this was beneficial from a financial point of view, it just made the embarrassment of losing at home to a non-league side even worse. Our league form up to the Cup exit had been quite reasonable, but following the humiliating Woking defeat, our league form nose dived and we slid alarmingly down the table.

In January, 1997, we travelled to Stockport where the Lions were tom apart by a rampant Stockport team. We were in the seats and noticed a firm of about a dozen Millwall boys enter the ground just after kick-off. They were closely followed by a group of plain clothed London policemen. This was not a covert police operation - instead they were letting Millwall know that they were being followed. This obviously had not prevented these boys from having a good drink though because they all looked the worse for wear.

The main stand was peculiar at Stockport because the toilets were in the away end and the food and drink bar was in the home end. Stockport had a few boys in this stand and every time they wanted to go to the toilet, they had to come into the away end. Likewise, if we wanted something to eat, we had to go into their end. The problems this could have caused were obvious, but instead of coming to blows in the ground, the rival factions arranged to meet in a pub in the town after the game.

Stockport scored their fifth goal early in the second half and this was the signal for most Millwall supporters to leave the ground. Millwall headed for the pub, closely followed by the London police. Although a couple of Stockport boys tried to get things organised, they soon dropped their bottle when they discovered that a few of the Millwall boys were tooled up. As a result of this and the obvious police presence, nothing really had happened. However, the intention had been there.

On the 30th of January, 1997, it was announced that Millwall had called in the administrators. It was a huge blow to all Millwall fans, but still came as no real surprise to anyone. The club had been mismanaged for years by a bunch of incompetent fools. The hope now was that heads would roll and the administrators would put the club back on an even keel. However, we desperately needed someone to invest in the club, and for a time there was a real possibility that the club could fold. It was a worrying time for all Millwall fans, but what annoyed me most was the attitude of the directors. They had failed to heed the warnings given to them by fans for years in an almost arrogant way. They thought they knew best because they were money men and we were just football fans. Well, Reg Burr, the fans knew best all along, and you should never forget you were the man who nearly brought our club, not your club, to its knees.

The next home game after the administration announcement was against Bristol City. Feelings were running high anyway as a result of the recent events, but any game against Bristol City is a big one for the Millwall boys. The fans of both teams have long hated each other and there have been a number of serious incidents in recent years. In 1985, 250 Millwall fans, many armed with pick axe handles, attacked a pub in Bristol used by their boys. On another occasion, City fans arriving at The Den were diverted to derelict wasteland where they were attacked by Millwall fans armed with CS gas canisters. Signs leading the coaches to the ground had been changed by one of the Millwall boys and the Bristolians had fallen for the scam. And at almost every other game between the two sides since the mid Eighties, there has been some sort of an incident involving fans of both teams.

This game was no exception and City brought their usual firm to Millwall. They baited the Millwall fans throughout the game with chants of "Millwall's going bust!", and with our players producing yet another pathetic performance, the Millwall fans finally lost their temper. Fans from all over the ground invaded the pitch, one fan even trying to attack Jimmy Nicholl. As is usual in these circumstances, the invaders headed towards the away end to confront the away fans. This was a little pointless seeing as the City fans were stuck in the top tier and had no way of getting onto the pitch.

Eventually, the Millwall fans returned to the stands to watch the rest of the match. After the game, some Millwall fans went over to Paddington in an effort to confront their boys. This is quite unusual, but not unheard of. Many Millwall fans do not like chasing away fans to Euston, Kings Cross, or Paddington because if you are arrested the police can prove intent on the grounds that you are in a mob somewhere you have no reason to be.

On this day, they saw a group of boys and asked them who they supported. One of the boys replied in a thick West country accent that he was City. This was enough for the Millwall, and the fan was cut across the face. I did not see this incident, but as I understand it, these boys were Exeter City fans, and not from Bristol at all. Whilst not condoning the actions of the Millwall supporters, the Exeter fans really should be more careful what they say in situations such as this.

Our rapid decline escalated and Millwall found themselves in real danger of getting relegated for a second consecutive season. Drastic measures were called for, and at last, Jimmy Nicholl had the decency to resign after the Bristol game. This decision was followed by the rapid departure of his star signings from Raith Rovers.

John Docherty returned to Millwall as temporary manager. This was a strange decision as Docherty had been out of football for a long time as a result of serious illness. Although he had managed Millwall in our most successful period ever, he had later been sacked by the club and subsequently sacked by Bradford City too, where I understand he was one of the most unpopular managers they have ever had. What's more, Docherty was a long ball merchant, and Millwall did not really have the players to accommodate this style of play. Despite my complete dislike of Jimmy Nicholl, at least he had tried to get Millwall to play good attacking football. The problem he had was that the players were simply not good enough to play good attacking football.

When a new manager turns up at a club, results often improve, probably as a result of the players trying to impress the new boss. Our results did improve, although the football was hardly attractive. However, under the circumstances, it was the results that counted, not the style of play.

On the 22nd of February me and two mates travelled to Shrewsbury to watch a boring 0-0 draw. Shrewsbury is a lovely town perched on the banks of the river Severn. Despite the picturesque surroundings and the embarrassing name of their ground, they do have a useful little firm and quite a few Millwall made the trip to Shropshire. Inside Gay Meadow, most of their boys were standing to our right. A couple of idiots in the Millwall end believed they could wind up the Shrewsbury fans by chanting England songs and

97

anti-Welsh songs whilst mimicking the sound of sheep. They thought they were hilarious, but instead of winding the home fans up, they really just embarrassed themselves. They obviously did not understand that most English boys who live in border towns such as Hereford, Shrewsbury and Carlisle are fiercely patriotic.

The three of us left the ground early, but as we left the car park, we were stopped by the police. "Were you the boys fighting in the pubs before the game?", they asked.

We had not been involved in any trouble, but even if we had been we would have to be pretty thick to fall for this line of questioning. Fortunately, we managed to bluff our way past the local constabulary without being fitted up or our names being added to the local pub watch scheme.

The Second Division was fairly tight that season, and with our recent upturn in form we stood a remote chance of reaching the play-offs. Another team with an outside chance was Burnley, and the two teams faced each other at Turf Moor in early April in a game which had a touch of importance about it. Judging by the performance of both teams though, you would have thought they were playing a pre-season friendly. It was a crap game played by two teams with serious attitude problems. I have seen this kind of performance many times before, but this really pissed me off that day because I had made the effort to travel a long way to watch my team. Burnley can be a very dodgy place for away fans and I was putting myself in danger of getting a good kicking just so I could watch the players run aimlessly around a football pitch for 90 minutes.

A couple of weeks later we went to Saltergate to see the Lions take on Chesterfield. Once again, Millwall were terrible and John Docherty was getting untold stick from the Millwall fans. He really should never have come back to the Den. If he hadn't, he would always have been fondly remembered by everyone as the man who guided Millwall to unimaginable heights. Instead, I will always remember him for overseeing some of the worst displays I have ever seen from a Millwall side.

I enjoyed the day at Saltergate though because the town was buzzing seeing as Chesterfield had reached the Semi Final of the FA Cup. It was a remarkable achievement for a small town club and everyone wished them well. I met many Chesterfield fans that day and was impressed by their friendliness. They had a huge mob in the seats next to us, but as there were only a few Millwall in the seats (and certainly no firm), they did not bother starting anything and earned my respect because of this. I felt a bit sorry for them when they were cheated out of the FA Cup a few weeks later.

The last home game of the season was against local rivals, Gillingham. As is always the case, the Gills brought a large and noisy following with them. They never cause any trouble at the Den, but always offer their team good vocal backing. At the end of the game, hundreds of Millwall steamed onto the pitch as is the custom at many clubs on the final day of the season. On this occasion, nearly all of the invaders were under twelve years old and it was really quite amusing to see them acting as if they were mad hooligans. The Gills fans and the police just laughed at the teeny terrors, but the press failed to see the funny side of it. This invasion was widely condemned by the media, who conveniently forgot to mention countless other pitch invasions that had occurred all over the country.

I always love the final day of the season, especially if the game is away from home. We were at Bury this year and they had just secured promotion to the First Division. Gigg Lane was going to be a sell out so I could not wait for this game. We spent the lunchtime drinking in Manchester with some United fans who were watching United play Leicester on Sky TV. Never let it be said that Manchester is run by City fans. United are the best supported team in the land and it is true to say that they have a lot of support all over the country. However, they also have a large fan base in Manchester despite what you may hear elsewhere. I think this is just a lie spread around by City fans who want to make City sound like a bigger club than they actually are.

We got carried away drinking with the United fans and by the time we left the pub in Manchester at ten to three, we could barely stand. A cab took us to Bury where hundreds of home fans were locked out. They were all really pissed off when we got out of the cab and walked straight into the away end. You could hear them muttering to the club officials about letting in away fans instead of home fans. I found this a bit of a liberty really because Bury are hardly the best supported club in the country. I bet the fans who were locked out had hardly been to a game during the lean years, but now that Bury had achieved a little success they wanted a seat on the bandwagon.

Bury won the game 2-0, and under normal circumstances I would have left the ground early to continue my end of season drinking frenzy. However, the Bury fans were all congregating at the front of the stand, obviously preparing to invade the pitch at full time and I wanted to see what would happen. The police got wind of what was going on and so it was announced over the tannoy that all Bury fans should return to their seats. I could not believe my eyes when they all did as they were told and returned to their seats like naughty school boys who had been told off by a teacher. This was supposed to be a group of northern football fans, all out on the piss together to celebrate being promoted, and yet they were being told what to do by a bunch of stewards. We all laughed at the sight of these northern mummy's boys as they quietly watched their team go up. Certainly, if and when Millwall ever get promoted, I can assure you that everyone at Millwall will celebrate in style and not be dictated to by club officials, the stewards, or the police.

Shortly after the end of the 1996/97 season, our new chairman, Theo Paphitis, announced that Billy Bonds would take over as the new manager of Millwall. This was the same Billy Bonds who was a living legend at Upton Park. What Millwall needed was a Millwall man, the sort of man who understands the passion within the club, and it was staggering to think that a West Ham man could run Millwall.

To be fair to Bonzo, he was a good, strong man who would not put up with nonsense from any of the players. In many ways, he was admired by many people because he was always a loyal, hard working and wise man. The only problem was that he was also a West Ham man. No matter how well he may do at Millwall, a large section of the crowd would simply hate him because of his association with our bitter rivals. Any Millwall manager needs the full support of the fans if he is to stand any chance of success. Poor old Bonzo never really stood a chance and for this reason alone, he should never have been appointed. Things got even worse when he appointed another Iron, Patsy Holland, as his assistant and brought in former Hammers, Paul Allen and Kenny Brown. Within the space of a couple of months we had turned into a retirement home for discarded Irons.

The 1997/98 season kicked off with a convincing 3-0 destruction of London rivals, Brentford. Considering it was the first game of the season, Brentford brought a terrible support with them to the Den. If only 600 or so could be bothered to travel ten miles to see their team on the first day of the season, things must be really bad at Griffin Park. Millwall played with a passion not seen for ages and quite a few people put their initial reservations about Bonzo's credentials behind them as they toasted victory after the game.

We were brought back down to earth on the Tuesday after the win though, losing 2-1 at Northampton in the League Cup. The following Saturday, we lost 2-1 at Preston despite a fantastic goal by Richard Sadlier. Preston is always a naughty place to visit and this game was marred by some serious incidents outside the ground.

The second leg of the League Cup came against Northampton at the Den ended up going to penalties. Millwall won the shoot out 2-0 in a comprehensive display of clinical finishing, reminiscent of Germany in Italy during the 1990 World Cup and Euro '96.

The season was plodding along in fairly unspectacular fashion. The highlight of a visit to Grimsby in September was when the two of us were pulled over by the local police as we approached the turnstiles. They had noticed a Stone Island badge on a jumper I was wearing and wanted to know if this meant I was a Millwall Bushwhacker. I asked one of them why he would think that, and he replied that he had noticed quite a few other Millwall supporters sporting the same badge. I explained to this bewildered, failed fisherman that the badge was a fashion symbol and nothing else. He did not comprehend the idea of fashion and seemed to think we should all be wearing bar scarves and woolly hats.

In October, we faced Watford at Vicarage Road in a top of the table clash. About 4,000 Millwall fans made the short journey to a much improved Vicarage Road. Millwall beat the Hornets 1-0 in a game that was played out in a fantastic atmosphere, with the Millwall supporters really getting behind their team that day. After the game, we walked miles back to the station through the town centre. When we passed a Whetherspoons pub in the town, a number of their boys came out of the pub in a bid to scare us. How can you be scared of a mob of lads who drink in a Whetherspoons pub? Watford are a family club, always have been and always will be, despite what certain authors may try to claim. They are no good at playing at being football hooligans and I would advise them not to even try.

The following week, Wigan turned up at the Den and played out a boring 1-1 draw. They brought a lively mob with them though and caused a lot of trouble around London Bridge and Borough High Street. Word soon spread and many Millwall put the return fixture down in their diaries as a must go to.

The game at Gillingham was the usual fun and games. The pubs are always shut in the town on match day so Millwall always get off the train at Chatham or Rochester. On this occasion, we chose Chatham and stayed in the pub opposite the station. There was no one else around, just Millwall fans drinking in this pub. The pub was soon surrounded by police who were recording anyone entering or leaving the pub. When we all left the pub to head to the ground, the police panicked and started ordering back-up. I don't know what they thought we were going to do because apart from a few minor incidents in the home end, there was no real trouble at all.

Fulham played at the Den in a mid-week clash a few weeks after in a game I had been looking forward to all season. They did not bring as many fans as I thought they would though, and the night turned into a bit of an anti-climax.

In the First Round of the FA Cup, we were drawn away at Bristol City in a potentially explosive game. City were romping away with the league and seemed certain to beat us. About 900 Millwall went to Ashton Gate, a disappointing turn out considering it was the FA Cup. About 150 boys caught the early train to Bristol and arrived at eleven o'clock. The police were waiting for them and had a plan of action. They took the Millwall fans to a pub near the ground and locked them in for the lunchtime session. Surely there was a better way of controlling the situation than this, because as kick-off time approached, the police unlocked the doors and allowed 150 pissed up Millwall boys to enter the ground. Sure enough, the fans kicked it off shortly after the game itself kicked off, ripping up seats and fighting the police. After the game, City were waiting for Millwall, as they always do, but Millwall just steamed straight into them, scattering the locals all over the park.

In December, we faced two more trips to the West Country in the space of a week. The first was an Auto Windscreen Cup game at Cardiff. Under normal circumstances, this game would be like World War Three as Cardiff have one of the largest and most violent mobs in the country. However, the Auto Windscreen Cup is pretty pointless (unless you reach the final) and only 1,219 fans turned up for the game. Millwall took a mob of 30 or so boys to Wales for this game and arrived early in the afternoon. They spent the afternoon drinking in the town, but as they made their way to the ground they were stopped by the police and put on the train back to London.

On the Saturday, we travelled to Plymouth, another club with a handy firm. A few Millwall supporters were drinking in a pub near the station before the game when suddenly a mob of local boys entered. To be fair to the Plymouth lads, they knew that this was not a firm and instead of picking on innocent fans, they told the supporters that if Millwall did have a firm that day, they should come back to the pub after the game. This is the way it should be at football. If you don't come across the other firm, there is no justification for attacking innocent fans. Unfortunately, this does not always happen, so I have a lot of respect for Plymouth. They often turn up at England away games, and always bring a good away following with them in the league, despite the long distances involved.

This season was turning into one of the most boring in living memory. The games at the Den were so dull, I was often tempted to stay in the pub. The away games were good in so much that you could have a good drink somewhere different. In January and February, we visited York and Oldham, two of the most friendliest places I have ever been to.

Oldham was absolutely freezing and the two of us were wrapped up especially well for the occasion in large Henry Lloyd coats. When we arrived at Oldham station, we asked an Oldham fan directions to a pub and he offered to take us to the pub he used before the games. We walked into the pub and walked into a time warp. The people in the pub looked like they had stepped out of a 1960s TV drama. They probably thought we were the odd ones out, but I have to say they were friendly and made us feel very welcome. I asked the barman for a bottle of lager and he said he knew he had one somewhere. He went off searching for this bottle and eventually returned with a can of Red Stripe which was the best he could offer.

The game itself was crap (as usual) and we left after 17 minutes. By now, it was snowing and so we were fully hooded up. We found a taxi firm and walked up the stairs to the office to ask for a cab to take us back to Manchester. The Pakistani sitting at the desk shit his load when he saw two hooded up young men with Southern accents enter his office. He instantly thought it was a raid and looked as if he was about to have a heart attack.

He was mightily relieved when we asked for a cab. We were back in Manchester by four o'clock when we met a mob of West Brom boys. They had been to Maine Road to watch the Baggies play Man City, but had the same idea as us and decided to get pissed rather than watch a pile of shit play football in the snow.

In March, we played Fulham at Craven Cottage. Millwall had sold out their allocation of tickets and four of us travelled to the game, one without a ticket. We arrived at the Cottage late as once again we had got carried away in the pub, this time watching Arsenal beat Man United in the live Sky game. My mate failed to buy a spare ticket and so decided to slip the turnstile operator a tenner. Mr Al Fayed's millions obviously don't pay the turnstile operators too much because he was only too happy to slip the extra money into his back pocket.

Tony Witter was sent off, but this had the opposite effect that it should have and Millwall played excellently. A fine victory was achieved when our former England international, Andy Gray, scored a spectacular winner. The poor boys from the wrong part of town had stuffed their wealthy rivals with only ten men, and the fans loved it, absolutely loved it.

Our final away game of the season was at Wigan. After the trouble they had caused at Millwall earlier on in the season, rumours were flying around that Millwall would take a good firm up North. The potential for violence was huge and the police were obviously aware of the rumours because it was suddenly announced that the game would be moved to the Friday night. No explanation was given, but none was really needed. Everyone knew why the game had been moved.

To travel to Wigan on a Friday night meant a day off work and the added expense of a hotel. This was enough to put some people off making the journey, but even so, Millwall took a good mob to Wigan, with many fans planning to spend the weekend in Blackpool.

The Millwall fans who travelled to the game by train were met by a large police presence fully kitted out in riot gear. I don't know what they expected, but they seemed to be prepared for a full scale riot. The Wigan boys were well up for it as well, and ended up fighting with the police in an effort to get at the Millwall fans. Had the game been played on the Saturday, I have no doubt there would have been major trouble, so in many ways, whoever made the decision to switch the game was proved correct. Even on the Friday night, there was still a lot of trouble, but it was mainly Wigan fans and the police involved in the disturbances, rather than Wigan and Millwall. Wigan fans fighting the police before and after the game though does not excite the media in the same way that Millwall fans fighting the police seems to do, so the events that went on that night were not reported in the media. No surprise there, then.

This boring season ended with a boring home game against Bournemouth. Roll on 1998/99!

CHAPTER 9

Shortly after the end of the 1997/98 season, Billy Bonds was sacked as Millwall's manager. It is true that the previous season had not been much of a success, but I think Bonzo had done a reasonable job, considering the circumstances. You have to appreciate that he came to a club in dire financial trouble, inherited a large squad of overpaid and over rated players, and on top of all that, the majority of Millwall fans disliked him because of his past association with the Irons.

Bonzo was given an impossible task, but appeared to be going about it in the right way. Given a little time he may have gone on to do well at Millwall. Despite their initial reservations, most Millwall fans had given Bonzo the benefit of the doubt and had treated him fairly throughout his time at Millwall. Although a few anti-West Ham comments were made from time to time, most genuine fans were so desperate for some sort of success that they were willing to forgive his past misdemeanours.

His assistant, Steve Gritt, had not been sacked and so it seemed natural to promote him to first team manager. Gritt had previously performed miracles at Brighton, managing to keep the South Coast club in the league against all odds. He also had a wide knowledge of the players in the lower and non leagues and seemed to me to be the ideal replacement.

It came as a bit of a surprise then when I read the newspapers and discovered that Keith "Rhino" Stevens and Alan McLeary had been appointed as manager and assistant manager respectively. This was a brave decision by the chairman, but one that could backfire on him if things did not work out. Rhino was and still is a legend to all Millwall fans, right up there with the likes of Barry Kitchener and the late Harry Cripps. He had spent his whole playing career at The Den, playing in various positions in the heart of our defence.

He was not exactly in the Bobby Moore mould as a defender and was certainly not blessed with the immense natural ability of the great England captain, but he epitomised the spirit of the football club, battling against often superior opposition with incredible courage and a never say die attitude that cannot be matched by most modem day footballers. He loved the club just as much as any

Millwall fan did, and that is probably why he spent all his playing days at Millwall. Certainly, nothing to do with the fact that AC Milan never tried to sign him.

Alan McLeary had been a vital member of the 1988 Championship winning team, playing alongside Rhino in the centre of defence. He left Millwall in acrimonious circumstances after taking a lot of stick from the fickle crowd. John Docherty brought him back to The Den in 1996/97 and it did not take McLeary long to win over the crowd again. In many ways he was a similar player to Rhino, a real warrior who gave his heart and soul in every game.

Both of them had been fantastic servants to Millwall as players. Above all, they were Millwall men. By this, I mean they understood the passion and desire within the club and were prepared to stand their ground and defend the honour of our beloved club when attacked by our many enemies. Neither man would look out of place stood on the terraces with the boys, dressed in Armani jeans and Stone Island jerseys, although having said that, it has to be said that both of them are much uglier than your average Millwall fan.

All Millwall fans loved these men, Rhino in particular, for what they had done for Millwall as players. However, neither of them had any managerial experience and the job in hand was without doubt one of the hardest in the lower leagues. Millwall had a large squad of useless players who really did not give a toss about the club and there was no money in the kitty to bring in new faces. In fact there was no money in the kitty for anything.

Millwall fans demanded some sort of success and they demanded it quickly. Promotion, a play-off position, a good Cup run, or a day out at Wembley would suffice. Our demands were not unreasonable, but my fear was that if Rhino was to prove unsuitable for the needs of our club, would the fans turn against him, as they had done to so many others in the past? I know I could not face yelling abuse at Rhino in the same way I did to McCarthy and some of the others, but what would happen if Rhino was genuinely a shit manager? He would have to go, for sure, but it would be a very sad day for everyone concerned with the club.

Where Rhino lacked practical experience in management, he more than made up for it with attitude. He was just as desperate for success as all the fans were, but above all, he knew what Millwall was all about. The wasters were quickly discarded and young players were brought in from the youth teams. Players who were prepared to fight for the club and players who were proud to play for Millwall. For a while now, Millwall had been operating a successful youth academy and reports were coming through of young and talented players emerging. This academy was proving expensive to run and there was talk that it would have to be shut down. This would surely spell the end for the club. For a number of years, our policy had been to bring in ageing stars like Clive Allen in the hope that they would bring the experience needed to gain promotion. In actual fact, what they brought was a lazy, arrogant attitude, which filtered down to the young impressionable players. On top of this, they were earning thousands of pounds a week, money that Millwall simply did not have. And most importantly of all, they did not really care about Millwall or the supporters.

For once, we also had a chairman who was not blinded by his own ego. Theo Paphitis knew that the way forward rested on the success of the youth academy. Players would be brought into the first team who would be eager to play for the club and who wanted to make a name for themselves. None of these players were earning ridiculous sums of money and so our wage bill was reduced quite drastically. Historically, Millwall have always been a selling club and whilst it would be nice to believe that we could keep hold of our bright, young players, this is never going to happen in the real world. By selling one or two of the better players, enough cash would be generated to keep on running the academy so more young players could come through the ranks and Millwall could survive as a full time professional football club.

With things looking a little brighter, I was eagerly anticipating the start of yet another season. All football fans are the same, no matter how poor the previous season was because you always believe the new season will bring success. The fixture list was released and it was announced that our first game would be away at Wigan. Surely, this game would not be moved to the Friday night.

Unfortunately, I could not go to this game. A friend from Scotland had arranged to stay for the weekend and I thought it would be a little rude if I pissed off to Wigan for the day. Instead, I went to the Valley to watch Hearts play Charlton in a friendly game. I left the game early and returned to the pub to see that Millwall had clinched a 1-0 victory. An away win on the first day of the season. Surely now Rhino was going to steer us to promotion.

The first league game at the Den was against Wycombe Wanderers. We had played Birmingham at St Andrews during the week in the League Cup but I did not go to that game either. Excited at the prospect of my first Millwall game of the season, I had a good drink and enjoyed a good day out at the football. As usual at the Den for these sorts of games, there was no trouble at the ground. However, a lot of Millwall boys had taken to drinking near London Bridge train station after the game - for obvious reasons. London Bridge is a busy station and most away supporters going to Millwall by train have to go through London Bridge to get to South Bermondsey. In addition, most supporters going to Selhurst Park also have to travel through London Bridge. On this day, Spurs were playing Wimbledon at Selhurst Park and as usual for London derby matches involving Wimbledon, most of the people attending the game were away fans.

After the game, a lot of Spurs fans had to change trains at London Bridge and surprise, surprise, Millwall were waiting for them. Spurs have always had a good mob, but traditionally there has not been a large rivalry between Spurs and Millwall, although this is not to say that it has never kicked off between the two sets of fans. Nonetheless, it all kicked off on this occasion, and for a while Borough High Street was closed to traffic while the police brought the situation under control. They did so by letting the police dogs attack the Millwall supporters, and a number of Millwall fans were caught and arrested.

Our next big game was away at Stoke in September. This was the first time Millwall had played at the new Britannia Stadium and so quite a few Millwall fans made the journey to the Potteries. My friend and I drove to Stoke and managed to secure a parking space right outside the away end, courtesy of a moody disabled sticker. It was ironic to see quite a few other "crippled" Millwall fans hobbling out of their cars, but the police just laughed at us. They laughed even louder when the Millwall coach driver reversed into a wall.

I had a few beers in the ground, and shortly after kick-off the majority of our mob entered the stadium. It turned out that they had been drinking in a pub in the town and Stoke had phoned the pub to let Millwall know that Stoke knew where they were. This was supposed to terrify the Millwall supporters so much that they would drink up and leave the area. If Stoke knew where Millwall were drinking, they should have come down to the pub to confront them instead of making idle threats over the telephone. This mob of

Millwall carried on drinking and eventually walked all the way to the ground without bumping into any Stoke boys.

Millwall played Stoke off the park, but in the final minute Stoke scored the winning goal. Suddenly, their fans appeared in the stand to our right and started giving it the big one. It's all very well doing that in the ground after scoring an undeserved winning goal, but they really should have been in the town before the game carrying out the dire threats they had made over the telephone.

Disappointed with the result, we drove home without any trouble. I later heard that some Millwall supporters had clashed with Man United fans on a train that evening in one of the most serious incidents of football related violence reported so far that season.

One good thing about the Second Division in 1998/99 was the fact that so called Northern giants, Manchester City, had finally been relegated the previous season. For years, Man City have been a shit club with shit players and shit managers. For some reason, their fans not only think they are the number one club in Manchester, but also one of the largest clubs in the country. To be fair to them, most of their fans have remained loyal over the years and their average attendances have remained fairly high. Having said that, they play in one of the largest urban areas in the United Kingdom and in a city that only has one other football club. Therefore, you would expect them to have a large support.

City have always had a large hooligan element amongst their support and firms such as the Maine Line Crew and the Young Guvnors had built up a fairly nasty reputation over the years. When they had finally been relegated at Stoke on the last day of the season these fans went on the rampage big time. Had it been Millwall fans rampaging like they did we would have been crucified, but this went largely unreported in the media.

It was obvious that Man City would still take hordes of fans with them to away games in Division Two. The potential for violence was immense as there was a number of teams with active firms in this league. Teams like Blackpool, Wigan, Preston, Burnley and Stoke would all be waiting for the arrival of the Mancs. Likewise, every club would take a good away following to Maine Road and the standard of policing at Maine Road has always been poor.

Down at the Den, we were due to play Man City on Saturday, the 5th of September. I had already booked a holiday for that weekend and resigned myself to missing the big game. I had been so desperate to see how many Mancs would actually come down to the Lions' Den and was absolutely gutted at the prospect of missing it. Luckily for me, the game was moved to a mid-week date because some players had to play for their international teams that weekend.

In the weeks building up to the game, Man City fans posted messages on the internet bragging about what they were going to do to Millwall supporters at this game. A few weeks before the game, many of them were involved in running battles with the Burnley Suicide Squad in the streets surrounding Maine Road. It was clear that Man City still had a large mob and many Millwall fans expected trouble at this game. I do not condone violence, but I believe if a mob of geezers are threatening to do all sorts to you, you have to meet fire with fire. If you live by the sword, you die by the sword and if things don't go your way, you should not moan about the consequences afterwards.

Before the game, all the pubs at Millwall and around London Bridge were packed full of Millwall boys waiting for the arrival of the Mancs. The mood was one of anger and lots of people wanted to teach these mouthy idiots a lesson they would never forget. Before the game though, no Mancs turned up and so everyone made their way to the ground. City had only brought 1,900 fans to the Den, but they barely raised a sound all night. The noise coming from the home support was impressive and inspired the young Lions to produce a wonderful display. We pulverised the City defence all night and had two good goals disallowed. Eventually, we took a thoroughly deserved lead. Each time the ball hit the back of the net, a handful of kids ran onto the pitch from the South Stand. They jumped around in the penalty area for 30 seconds or so, then raced back into the stand before they could be ejected. No harm was done and no City players were assaulted.

Late on in the game, one of the City players launched a two footed tackle on Paul Shaw who instantly retaliated. Players from both sides converged on the two players and began pushing each other. It was a nothing incident that looked worse than it really was, the sort of incident that happens at a lot of games. The referee sent off two players and the game continued in the same heavy atmosphere.

In the final minute, Man City equalised and for a short while their fans woke up and offered a particularly weak rendition of *Blue Moon*. City had snatched a point in controversial fashion and most Millwall supporters left the ground in a very bad mood. Inevitably, the City fans were kept in the ground by the police after the final whistle. A large mob of Millwall supporters gathered outside, and when the police tried to disperse them they were met with a barrage of missiles. The usual sort of thing happened and the running battles continued for some time after the game. No Man City fans were involved in any of the trouble that surrounded this fixture, mainly because none of the so called Guvnors had the bottle to turn up at the Den.

Even although Millwall fans were to blame for all the trouble that occurred at this fixture, the City fans have to take some of the responsibility. Their fans had been bragging for ages about how they were going to invade towns and take liberties at grounds in Division Two. Well, the likes of Macclesfield or York may not be able to do anything to prevent City carrying out their threats, but down at Millwall we were never going to stand for that sort of nonsense. All these threats had just increased the amount of Millwall boys who were prepared to protect our ground from the mouthy Mancs. Whether we like it or not, Millwall do have a reputation for violence and it has to be said that some Millwall fans are proud of this reputation and will do anything they can to preserve it. Others, like me, do not really believe our own reputation, but if we are put in a position where we feel we are being threatened, we are prepared to stand up and be counted. Consequently, Millwall can get a huge mob of lads together if the circumstances are right.

After the game, Millwall were condemned by the press and the FA. Curiously, most of the attention surrounded the pitch invasions rather than the trouble outside. In a way this was good as the trouble outside had been very serious, but even the FA appreciate that Millwall can't do anything about what the fans get up to after they have left the ground. The pitch invasions themselves were fairly innocuous, just a bunch of over excited kids running onto the pitch to celebrate a goal.

The comments made after the game by Joe Royle were scandalous though. He claimed that if Man City had won, their players would not have got out of the Den alive. This was a load of bollocks and Royle had no reason to make such a stupid statement. He must have known that the media would pick up on this accusation and use it to full effect, which they most certainly did. He should have kept his mouth shut. As a football manager, his only comments should have been about the game and he should not have answered a hypothetical question about what might have happened had Man City won. To me, he was just inciting trouble ahead of the return game at Maine Road. This fixture needed no hype, as City fans would obviously be out to seek revenge in any case.

However, most Millwall boys were disappointed with what had happened that night. Our firm desperately wanted to get hold of the City firm and prove to them that they would not be allowed to take liberties just because they thought they were a big team in a lower league. Millwall turned up in numbers, but City had failed to do the same. Surely they would have to show at the return game at Maine Road. A fun day out in Moss Side loomed in the New Year.

Shortly after the Man City game, Fulham played at the Den and another large crowd filled the ground. Whenever a large crowd turns up, there is always potential for trouble, but fortunately this game went off relatively peacefully. The referee had a terrible game, making one bad decision after another, and in the last minute, Millwall once again conceded another goal, this time losing 1-0. At the final whistle, two fans invaded the pitch from the East Stand and headed towards a Fulham player. The stewards spotted the invaders and both of them were quickly apprehended.

In the press conference after the game, the media concentrated on this incident alone. Kevin Keegan was fuming. His team had just clinched yet another away win, but all the media wanted to do was to get him to stick the knife into the Millwall fans. They were desperate for a quote from Keegan that would make spectacular headlines, similar to the one they had quite easily managed to get from Joe Royle. Just imagine, a quote from Keegan saying how all Millwall fans are scum and the club should be closed down. The media would have loved it, really loved it.

Keegan responded to the questioning by pointing out the wonderful passion generated by the home crowd. He said the Den was clearly a place where the home fans cared deeply about their team. He did not have a bad word to say about Millwall and in my opinion he said something that was so obvious, I am surprised that other people have never said it before. He pointed out that as so many people cared passionately about Millwall, it was no surprise that every now and then a couple of people overstep the mark. Passion was going out of football and killing the sport. Therefore, it was good to see that passion still exists at the Den and this passion should never be allowed to die. Keegan hit the nail right on the head with his comments, but did not win any new fans in the media. Most of the journalists were disappointed that Keegan had failed to provide them with what they wanted to hear and chose not to print his comments in their newspapers.

Following the last minute defeat by Fulham, our next interesting game was in the First Round of the FA Cup in early November. This time we had been drawn away (again), this time to Swansea. I had visited the Vetch Field in 1991 for a Wales - England B international, but I had never been there for a Swansea match. I had heard all the horror stories of how visits to Swansea can be very dangerous for Englishmen and so I decided the trip needed careful planning. I either had to go with a mob and be prepared for trouble or I had to think of somewhere safe to drink. After much deliberation, I chose the latter option and booked up the train tickets. I was due to arrive in Swansea at 10:30am and had decided that if a good mob was on this train me and my mate would stick with them. If no boys were on this train, we would jump in the first taxi we found and go over to the Mumbles village for a quiet drink.

All my plans went pear-shaped when it was announced that the game had been moved to the Friday night. Once again, no explanation was given. I could not travel on the Friday, and much to my disgust, Great Western Trains refused to give me a full refund. On the night of the match, my mood turned even angrier as Swansea ripped Millwall apart, finally running out winners by three clear goals.

Despite the fact that the game was on the Friday night, I still expected trouble at this match. I saw the goals on TV on Saturday lunchtime and noticed that Millwall had a mob of about 30 boys in the seats and a total of about 300 fans in the ground. I did not think this mob was large enough to turn Swansea over on their own manor and as there had been no reports of trouble in the press, I assumed the night had passed by peacefully.

The following week I went to the Den for the Bristol Rovers game and heard numerous stories from some of the fans who had made it to Swansea. There had been trouble in city centre pubs before the game as mobs of locals had gone from pub to pub in search of Londoners. Inside the ground, the atmosphere had been very hostile and our black players were subjected to serious racial abuse. And as the Millwall supporters left the ground, they were attacked by a huge mob of Swansea fans. By all accounts, the trouble had been quite serious; innocent fans had been hurt and players and fans racially abused. None of these events were reported in the media. I wonder what would have happened if the shoe had been on the other foot. I guess that if Swansea fans had been attacked at Millwall and their players subjected to racial abuse, the headlines would have dominated the papers for days. It seems that it is only when Millwall fans cause trouble that the violence is reported.

I am not moaning at the behaviour of the Swansea fans. We live in a violent world and Swansea has long had a reputation in football circles for being a particularly dangerous place to visit. Millwall supporters have dished out their fair share of beatings over the years and what goes around comes around. Fair play to Swansea. The point I am making is that the press were at the game, but because Millwall fans were not responsible for the trouble they felt there was no point in reporting the violence. After all, Millwall players and fans are never victims, are they?

In December, Cardiff visited the Den in an Auto Windscreen Cup match. Maybe there is something in the water down in South Wales, but everyone knows that Cardiff have one of the most violent followings in Britain. God knows what a South Wales derby is like. Anyway, a few Millwall boys are friendly with some of the Cardiff lads and so phone calls were made and arrangements for a meet discussed. This often goes on at football and is something most people cannot understand. If you are mates with someone, it seems logical to meet up and have a drink before the game. What actually happens is that you will arrange for you and your mates and him and his mates to meet in a pub somewhere to fight each other. The people who do not understand this mentality fail to understand that these people actually *enjoy* the fighting and all the excitement that goes with it. The buzz and the rush of adrenalin that you feel can last for days. If all of them enjoy fighting, then it seems reasonable for them to meet up so they can get on with what they enjoy doing. I appreciate that this type of behaviour is difficult to understand for outsiders, but the fact is it does go on. I am no expert on why people behave as they do and I am not searching for any clever answers either. I will leave that up to the so called experts at Leicester University. What I will say is that you should not criticise what you don't understand.

Two coach loads of boys came up from Cardiff that evening and made various phone calls to their friends in the pub at Millwall as their journey progressed. Eventually, Cardiff turned up, but the big fight failed to materialise, probably as a result of a determined police presence. Should the two teams meet in the league however, the police will have a momentous task to prevent literally thousands of people from both sides indulging in their favourite pastime.

Christmas came and went without anything too exciting happening. By now, the talk at Millwall was of the game at Maine Road. Every man and his dog was planning on making the trip, but my experience told me not to believe everything that was being said. A few weeks before the game it was announced that the match would be all ticket. Prices for tickets in the away end were £16. I know City think they are big time, but they should never forget that this was a Second Division match being played in a run down ground. How could they justify charging Millwall supporters £16 when just a few weeks earlier they had charged Fulham fans just £12? A call to Maine Road indicated that the prices had apparently been increased to cover the additional expenditure for extra policing and stewarding.

Despite the extortionate price of the tickets, the 2,400 tickets we had been allocated went like hot cakes and were sold almost immediately. It appeared that everyone who had been bragging about making the trip had been genuine after all. Millwall Football Club made it clear that fans should not travel to the game without a ticket as they would be refused entry to the ground.

I booked my APEX tickets with Virgin trains and was allocated a seat on the 07:45am train out of Euston, due to arrive in Manchester at 10:30am. On my previous visits to Manchester, I had always caught this train as it gives you time to have breakfast in a cafe and find a pub ready for opening time. This time things were going to be different. There was no way that the city centre would be a safe place to drink, especially when you take into account the fact that United fans would be in the vicinity of the station, as they were only playing away at Nottingham Forest that day. I felt that if the Mancs were not picking fights with Millwall supporters they would most certainly be fighting each other. I had thought of jumping in a cab and finding a quiet pub somewhere, but if I chose this option, I was still open to danger. First and foremost, I could be spotted as a Southerner and attacked, or secondly I might get caught up in the expected battle between City and United fans.

Most Millwall fans were booked on the 07:45, 08:45 and 09:45 trains out of London, arriving in Manchester at 10:30, 11:30 and 12:30 respectively. The word on the street was that everyone should get off at Stockport, and once everyone was together, travel into Manchester in numbers. This suited me down to the ground. I did not really want trouble and knew I would be safer if we all stuck together. If it did kick off, we would have a better chance of protecting ourselves.

I arrived at Euston early that morning and instantly recognised many Millwall fans. One thing that struck me was the distinct lack of police in the station. No doubt they were keeping an eye on the fans from their vantage point in the offices overlooking the concourse, but it may have been a little better, from their point of view, to let Millwall know they were being watched. About 200 Millwall fans boarded the train, and to be honest, most of the lads on this train were just normal fans. Although they were not wearing colours, they were not dressed in a casual way either, many of them just wearing normal sportswear such as Nike sweatshirts. There were just various small groups of lads, drinking and having a laugh. They were probably aware of the dangers that lay ahead, but I do not think they were actively looking for trouble or even that concerned about the prospect of trouble. There were a number of casuals, dressed in the usual attire of Armani jeans and Stone Island jackets. Most of the casual lads on the train were slightly younger, about 19 or 20, but there were a few older boys as well. I spoke to a few of them who confirmed that everyone was meeting in Stockport. Most of the main boys were on the two later trains and it was felt that once everyone was in Stockport, the main boys would get things going.

As the train pulled in at Stockport, I was surprised to see only two police officers on the platform. I was sure that the Manchester police would have received intelligence from the Met that Millwall were planning on drinking in Stockport before the game and would have taken steps to cope with this. It had been no secret in South London that this was the plan, so either the police have no intelligence or they chose to let us drink in Stockport. Maybe they wanted Millwall in Stockport, away from the mean streets of Piccadilly and Moss Side.

The train pulled to a stop and 200 Millwall fans alighted. The two policemen appeared to be in a state of shock at the sight of 200 young men converging on Stockport at ten o'clock on a Saturday morning. As I passed the two officers, they were frantically speaking into their walkie-talkies and I heard one of them say, "I've never seen nothing like it."

This made me chuckle - after all there were another two train loads of boys due to arrive in the next two hours, and the boys on those trains were no mugs whatsoever. The 200 of us walked up the hill to the roundabout. Our main problem was the fact that it was an hour until opening time and there are not many attractions in Stockport for 200 young men to amuse themselves with for an hour on a Saturday morning. We were all stood in the road discussing what to do and where to go, oblivious to the fact that we were causing a traffic jam. The funny thing was, not one car hooted at us.

It was decided we would split up and meet back at the roundabout for eleven o'clock. There were two pubs next to each other by this roundabout and another three pubs within 100 yards down the main shopping street. As such, there would be no problem getting a drink. I found a bookies and sat in there for an hour, wasting my money. At eleven o'clock, a pub called the Irish Bar opened, and we went in, closely followed by a few other Millwall fans. A local lad was in the bar and he was shocked to see so many Millwall fans in the pub at opening time. When we explained we were on our way to Man City, he wished us luck and told us to "do the blue bastards."

This was the largest of the five pubs and it quickly filled up with Millwall supporters. At about eleven o'clock, the second train pulled in and another 200 or so Millwall boys walked up the hill from the station and came into the pubs. The atmosphere in the pubs was great as old friends greeted each other. Faces you had not seen at Millwall for years were here, and it soon became apparent that we were going to have a huge mob today.

The third of the three trains arrived at noon, and amazingly all three trains had arrived on time. Once again, a couple of hundred Millwall walked up the hill and met their mates in the pubs near the roundabout. By now, police reinforcements had been drafted into Stockport and riot vans were positioned outside all five pubs, keeping an eye on the visitors.

Inside the Irish Bar, the ringing of mobile phones was relentless. A handful of Millwall had travelled into Manchester to check on who was around. They reported back that Man United had a mob of about 150 boys who had been drinking in the pubs in Piccadilly. They had been waiting to ambush the Millwall mob as they came out of Piccadilly. They now knew that Millwall were drinking in Stockport and had jumped on a train bound for Stockport to confront Millwall. It was also reported that City did not have a mob in the city centre, so we assumed they would be waiting in Moss Side.

About 20 minutes later, someone said they were here. Drinks were gulped down in one, and the Irish Bar emptied within seconds. We walked up the road to the roundabout at the top of the hill, along with the boys from the other pubs. At this stage, there was probably about 400 Millwall fans on top of the hill. At the bottom of the hill, the 150 Man United fans were coming out of the station. A deafening roar went up and Millwall charged down the hill. The United fans did not stand a chance and raced back to the safety of their train. The riot police were outside the station and they took the full brunt of the Millwall aggressors. Bottles and glasses were thrown at the police, but once Millwall had used their weapons, the police had the upper hand. They charged up the hill and ran Millwall back to the roundabout. Here, there was a tense stand off as the police blocked the road to the station. Another road appeared to lead to a back entrance to the station and a few Millwall raced down there, hoping to get at United. The police quickly got hold of them though and forced them back to the roundabout. The stand-off continued for a few minutes. Every now and then bottles were launched at the police, but they bounced off their riot shields without causing any damage.

A pub called the Jolly Crofter was just down the road from this roundabout and most of the top boys were in this pub. They had stayed in the pub when it had gone off, but were now out of the pub having a go at some of the Millwall boys. They were angry that it had gone off here because now the police would be on top of us all day and our chances of getting to the City firm would be slim.

These boys were correct, and after the situation calmed down the police escorted us to the station. The platform was packed with Millwall fans and riot police, and must have been an intimidating sight for the passengers on the train when it pulled into the station. I have to say, the faces of the passengers, particularly those wearing City shirts, was a picture. I managed to get a seat and found myself sat next to a City fan in his late teens. I asked him if he was going to the game. He had a City tracksuit on, but looked like he wanted to deny he was a fan of any football team let alone City. He relaxed when I made it clear I was only having a laugh with him, and reassured him that he was safe on this train.

He made me laugh when he said that he had got on the train at Macclesfield, and knowing that the train had come from London he was a bit worried that some Millwall fans might be on it. He had relaxed when he saw the train was virtually empty and was enjoying the quiet journey to Manchester until the train had pulled into Stockport and he was greeted with the sight of hundreds of angry Millwall fans surrounded by riot police. I told him that the police were bound to walk us to Maine Road and as he was now with us, he would be stuck with us for the rest of the day. This did not go down too well and for a moment I thought he was going to cry. Luckily for him, when we arrived at Piccadilly, the police let him go.

We were not so lucky though, and as expected, the police kept us together and walked us all the way to Maine Road. This was the heaviest police escort I had seen since the England fans had marched to the ground for the Holland game in the 1990 World Cup. Shortly after we had set off, the police stopped us. We could see a mob of boys up a side street, and at first I thought this was City fans trying to attack the escort. It soon became apparent that it was just another mob of Millwall and the police wasted no time bringing this wayward mob into the escort.

As we walked quietly through the wet streets of Manchester, I fully expected an ambush around every corner. We had been promised a hot reception by the City fans, and I for one thought they would be up for it. As we continued walking without seeing any threatening faces, my thoughts soon turned to my willy. I had drunk five or six pints in Stockport and was now bursting for a piss. Thankfully, the police stopped the escort to allow everyone to have a piss. Unfortunately, I am one of these sad people who can never pee in a crowd. Why, I don't know, but I never go for a piss at half-time because I usually stand there holding it while people come and go. Naturally, I get some strange looks, so now I always go during the game when the toilets are quiet. On this occasion though, I could not go on the pee break, and as we walked slowly to the ground, I felt excruciating pain all the way.

We approached Maine Road and finally saw some City fans. Where had they been hiding all afternoon? Over 600 Millwall fans marched through their manor without a peep from them. Amazing really, when you consider that Moss Side is supposed to be the English Bronx. These City fans started mouthing off at us, but Millwall just laughed at them, treating them with the contempt they deserved. If this was their idea of a hot reception, then they really should have turned up at Millwall. They would have seen what a hot reception really was.

I could not look menacing if I tried though, as I was bent double with six pints of lager bursting to come out of my willy. I pushed through the queue at the turnstiles and walked straight into the Gents. The relief was unimaginable and the pee seemed to last for hours. Feeling two stone lighter, I walked into the stand to find Millwall had been allocated half the North Stand. City fans occupied the other half and between us was a thin line of stewards. Everyone in football knew this was a high profile game. Millwall Football Club had warned Man City that trouble was likely and had urged them to take extra precautions. They even had the nerve to charge each Millwall fan an extra £4 to cover the cost of the additional security. Despite this, they had failed to escort the supporters coaches to the ground and now we found ourselves with just a line of stewards separating 5,000 rival fans. This is something that would never happen at the Den, and Man City really need to ask themselves why they did not take the necessary precautions to prevent trouble. Their negligence put every fan, steward and police officer at risk that day.

As the game kicked-off, the City fans made a half hearted attempt to create an intimidating atmosphere. In the bottom tier of the Kippax Stand, young City fans chanted abusive songs at us. With their silly hair cuts and even sillier dress sense, they looked like wannabe Noel Gallaghers and really were a comical sight. I should point out here that the notorious Gallagher brothers were conspicuous by their absence. For two Manchester hard men and diehard City fans, this was a little surprising. I appreciate they now live in London, but it only takes a little effort to make the journey to Manchester to see your beloved team. Seeing as how they could not even be bothered to go to the Den earlier on in the season, I should not have been so surprised. Apparently, that night they visited a film premier in the West End with their mum. The self styled wild men of rock'n'roll had really let themselves down. What would Ozzy Osborne say?

In the second half, City took the lead and this was the spark for it to go off in the North Stand. Throughout the game, both sets of fans had been verbally abusing each other and throwing missiles. As City scored and their fans were celebrating, a mob of Millwall charged through the line of stewards and into enemy territory. The City fans backed off and a few Millwall fans kicked arse until the police finally got it together. The police were not messing around either and slaughtered the Millwall fans. They were being extremely heavy handed and were lashing out at anyone with their batons. Many fans were hurt by the police, including one who was knocked unconscious. This just infuriated the bulk of the Millwall supporters and made the trouble even worse.

By now, the City fans were doing what they are good at. Behind a line of police, they were issuing threats about what they were going to do to us outside and throwing coins at us. Although the situation was becoming very dangerous, I had to laugh when I heard a Millwall fan complaining to a steward that pound coins were going over, but only pennies were coming back.

One thing that really annoyed me was when a message to the City fans in the North Stand came over the tannoy. Some stupid woman urged the City fans to ignore the trouble Millwall fans were causing and not to sink to our level. They were urged to remember the good name City have. When this message was heard, we were being attacked by the police, threatened by City fans, and bombarded by various missiles! None of this would have happened had it not been for the stupidity of Manchester City Football Club, and now, right at the wrong moment, they were blaming us.

Eventually, the police gained control of the situation in the stand, but with City scoring another two goals, there was bound to be further trouble outside. We were told we were to be kept in the ground for seven minutes after the final whistle, while the traffic congestion died down. I don't know why it takes exactly seven minutes for the traffic to leave the area, but we all knew the real reason we were being kept in. While we were safely locked in the ground, the brave City fans went on a rampage of their own. Three empty Millwall supporters' coaches were damaged and the driver of one of the coaches hospitalised. The ever helpful Manchester police had directed the coach drivers to park their coaches behind the home stand. Local shops and restaurants were also smashed. All this could be heard by us inside the ground, but still the tannoy announcer insisted we were being kept in as a result of traffic congestion.

After about half an hour we were advised that we could leave the ground. Over the tannoy it was announced that the situation outside was hostile and our safety could not be guaranteed. This was met by the largest cheer of the afternoon from the Millwall supporters. We left the ground under heavy police escort and started the long walk back to the station. The walk took about an hour and in all that time, not one Manchester City fan showed their face. We had been warned that we would be in extreme danger in Moss Side from mobs of angry Mancs. However, it appeared that they had released their anger by smashing a couple of windscreens and attacking one innocent coach driver. Even when we got to Piccadilly, no City fans were to be seen and the police managed to put us on a special train back to London without any further trouble.

This was a game where there was always going to be trouble, but the risk of violence increased as a direct result of negligence by Man City Football Club. Millwall took a huge mob of boys to this game, intent on trouble, and should accept part of the blame, yet the only trouble they encountered was with Man United fans in Stockport. This incident was over before it started as United realised they did not have a good enough firm to cope with over 500 Millwall boys. Inside the ground, the City fans did not really want to know, despite their provocative behaviour. If Man City fans had shown any real interest in fighting Millwall, this could have been one of the most violent games of the modem era. However, as it turned out, it really was not that bad. A few bottles thrown in Stockport, a brief fight in the stand during the game, and a few missiles thrown by both sets of fans. I know of two other football related incidents that occurred that day which were probably just as serious as what happened in Manchester and Stockport. In Swansea, a linesman was attacked by fans invading the pitch in the game between Swansea and Brighton. And once again, opposition players were subjected to racial abuse by Swansea fans. And outside Victoria Station in London, Birmingham fans returning from their game at Selhurst Park with Crystal Palace were attacked by a mob of Chelsea fans. Chelsea had played Southampton that day, and after the game a mob had travelled over to Victoria with the specific intention of fighting Birmingham. The pub in which the Birmingham fans were drinking was attacked three times by Chelsea fans, hell bent on hurting the Midlanders.

Unsurprisingly, these two events went unreported in the media. Meanwhile, most papers had dispatched two journalists to Maine Road - one was a sports writer to report on the game and one was a crime reporter to report on the expected trouble. Every little event was blown out of proportion by these reporters. Millwall fans were reported as rampaging through Stockport, when in actual fact we were greeted with open arms by the pubs in the town. The only trouble that erupted in Stockport was as a direct result of Man United fans arriving en masse to confront us. Most annoying of all was the fact that we were blamed for smashing the shops, restaurants and coaches around Maine Road. How we caused this trouble when we were locked in the ground, I will never know. I also fail to understand why we would want to smash our own coaches and hurt one of the drivers who was to take some of us home. Maybe Karen Brady was right when she said Millwall supporters are to blame for all the world's evils because we attract trouble and bring out the worst in others.

As I said, Millwall fans must hold their hands up and take part of the blame. As should Manchester City Football Club, City fans, United fans, Manchester police and Joe Royle. Royle was the idiot who made comments such as "We have a score to settle with Millwall", "They will get a hot reception at Maine Road", and "We nearly did not get out of the Den alive". Comments such as this are bound to increase tension in a game that really didn't need any build up. If Royle had made controversial comments about the performance of a referee, the FA would have had him up on a disrepute charge almost immediately. However, he appears to have carte blanche to say whatever he wants about another football club and its supporters without attracting any criticism from the FA or the media. Or maybe it's just Millwall that are fair game.

The Man City trip had brought back fond memories of the way football was in the Eighties when I had first started travelling to games. The casual clothes, the banter on the journey and in the pubs, the hostile atmosphere in the ground, and above all, the real possibility of it kicking off. In the Nineties, going to football has lost a lot of the raw excitement that was abundant in the Eighties. Luckily, Millwall play in the Football League and not in the glitzy Premiership. The Premiership seems to attract a different sort of character to grounds these days, and the atmosphere at some of our larger stadiums is incredibly dull. If the bubble does ever burst, and I for one sincerely hope it does, I wonder if all these new fans will continue to go to football. Hopefully, they will find other hobbies and leave the football to the lads from the housing estates throughout the country. Football has always been a sport for the working classes, but in the Nineties it has been hijacked by the middle classes.

The possibility of violence at football is an attraction for many people. Certainly, the majority of the 2,400 Millwall fans that made the long trip to Maine Road were not that upset that Millwall had suffered a heavy defeat. From a purely football point of view, the defeat was a bitter blow to our chances of gaining a play-off position, but this disappointment was nothing compared to the exhilaration felt by most of us as a result of the show of strength from our support.

This game in particular, and the culture of football related violence in general, was all about reputation. City fans had been boasting for months that Millwall were going to get a hiding in Manchester. If we had failed to show, we would never be able to boast about our reputation again. But with Millwall showing up in such force and taking diabolical liberties, with very little opposition from one of the most notorious firms in the country, it really was a great day to be a Millwall supporter.

The following week, we faced another mundane fixture, this time away to Lincoln. As I had never been to Sincil Bank, I was looking forward to this game, despite the fact that I knew it would be nothing like the previous awayday in Manchester. We drove to Lincoln and after a few beers in a pub on the edge of the town, we found ourselves in a pub on the High Street, opposite the ground. There were a few Lincoln boys in here and they soon deduced that we were Millwall supporters. Fortunately, they were a friendly bunch and wanted to find out exactly what had happened at the City game. They had a particular hatred for City after the way their fans had behaved at Sincil Bank, and they were pleased to hear that Millwall had given City a taste of their own medicine. These boys had been drinking in Manchester the previous week as Lincoln had played at Oldham, and were well aware of the size of mob we had taken. They were mightily relieved when I explained that our support today was likely to total only about 500, with only a small contingent of boys up for trouble.

As kick-off time approached, we left the pub with these boys and headed to the ground. Arrangements were made to meet them back in the pub just after half-time to continue our drinking session. Sure enough, it was another dire game and we found ourselves back in the pub by four o'clock. More drink was drunk and stories exchanged about previous awaydays. It really was a great afternoon, drinking in a pleasant town with some good lads. Everything about the day was entirely different to the City trip, but in its own way it had been just as enjoyable.

After the Lincoln game, Stoke were due to visit the Den the following Saturday for what is usually one of the best days of the season. Before that, we faced Gillingham in the Southern Area Semi-Final of the Auto Windscreen Shield. Although not the most glamorous tournament in the world, it does offer small clubs like Millwall a real chance of a trip to Wembley. The club had reduced the cost of admission to £5 for this game and a large crowd was expected. I arrived at the Den shortly before kick-off and was shocked to see hundreds of people struggling to gain admission. Wembley fever had gripped Bermondsey and a buzz of excitement was in the night air.

The size of the crowd had obviously shocked the club and even Gillingham fans had turned up in numbers. For this game, the club had arranged to shut the bottom tiers of the two main stands, an exercise designed to reduce the cost of policing and stewarding. Whilst this idea makes sense, it seems pointless to leave the bottom tier of the South Stand open. Anyone wanting to invade the pitch need only sit in this stand. In the past many of the fans who had invaded the pitch had done so from this end anyway. As it turned out, the bottom tier of the East Stand was eventually opened due to the size of the crowd.

The game itself was a tough, physical encounter, but our young lionhearts showed great spirit, although they found it difficult to break down the Gills defence. The game remained goalless and went into extra time where the golden goal rule meant that the next goal would win the game, a throwback to football matches we used to play at school. Incredibly, it was our cumbersome centre forward, Richard Sadlier, who snatched the crucial goal, which was enough to send Millwall into the Southern Area Final of the tournament.

Delirium swept the Den when the ball hit the back of the net. The magnitude of the joyous celebrations was incredible. People were singing and dancing for ages as suddenly the idea of a Wembley trip became a distinct possibility. I rushed back to the pub after the game and all the talk was of Wembley and how many fans we would take.

The excitement carried forward to Saturday as we awaited the arrival of our old friends from the Potteries. The pubs at Millwall were busy before the game, and once again Wembley was the talk of Bermondsey. As far as I was concerned, Wembley stories could be put on hold until we were actually there. Most of us had forgotten the small matter of the two leg Southern Area Final, and I for one was certain that Millwall would blow it, as they had done so often in the past.

I arrived at the Den, late as usual, to find out that Bobby Bowry had been sent off in the second minute, a decision that by all accounts was very dubious. The Stoke support was pathetic, and only about 600 had turned up. After their dismal showing at the Britannia Stadium, any respect I had held for Stoke in the past went out of the window, but it soon became obvious why their supporters were so disillusioned. Stoke were just about the worst side I have ever seen. Millwall had another player sent off, which meant we were down to nine men. The referee was diabolical and helped Stoke in any way possible, but despite this, Millwall won 2-0 and it really should have been by more. I even started to feel sorry for the genuine Stoke fans who had travelled to watch this shower of shit. It was a pathetic performance from a professional football team. Surprisingly, the Stoke fans just sat back and let their players get away with it. Maybe, they were used to such feeble displays, but I'd like to think if a Millwall team played as poorly as Stoke did, our supporters would not have put up with it. Footballers earn good money and are the envy of most young men. The least they should do is put in a little effort.

By now, Walsall had beaten Cambridge, to set up the Southern Area Final. The Northern Area Final was to be contested by Wrexharn and Wigan. Assuming Millwall would beat Walsall, I was hoping Wrexham would meet us at Wembley. I felt Wrexham would bring a larger support to London for the game, and the England - Wales rivalry would bring an added edge to the day.

The first leg of the Southern Final was at the Den. As expected, a large crowd turned up to cheer on the Lions. Walsall only brought 800 or so fans, but despite this, the atmosphere was alive from the first kick of the ball. It got even better when Millwall took an early lead, but this was also the spark for Walsall to take charge of the game. They dominated the game, hitting the woodwork and even missing a penalty. Fortunately, they failed to hit the net and the game ended in a 1-0 victory for the Lions. I felt that this slender lead would be difficult to protect in the return leg, and as far as I was concerned our Wembley dream was over.

However, where there is a will, there is a way, and I managed to secure some tickets for the second leg. Millwall had been allocated about 1,900 tickets, and they had sold like hot cakes. We made our way up the M6 to the delightful suburb of Walsall, just north of Birmingham. The ground, as with many of the new grounds that have been built over the last few years, was in the middle of a soulless industrial estate. This was my second visit to Walsall and I knew what to expect, but fortunately they do have a social club which normally caters for away fans for a small entrance fee, and we managed to get in there for our pre-match drink. As we were Millwall supporters though we could not be trusted with glasses, so our beer was served in those horrible plastic cups whilst the locals downed their pints of bitter from proper glasses. Is it really necessary to treat people in such a fashion? After speaking to some Walsall fans, they said this policy had been in place ever since some Birmingham fans had caused trouble in the social club at a pre-season friendly. To realise we were being punished for the actions of some stupid Blues fans just added salt to my wounds.

Before the game, I actually felt quite nervous. For obvious reasons, I desperately wanted Millwall to win, but being a born pessimist I had resigned myself to the fact that Millwall were bound to blow it. Walsall's performance at the Den had done nothing to quash my fears, and as I headed to the ground I was not too hopeful.

Once I pushed my way through the turnstiles, my mood soon changed. The noise coming from the away end was deafening. Although the away end was all seated, everyone was standing up and most of the fans were standing right at the front of the stand. The fans were not only getting behind the team, we were also making a determined effort to intimidate the referee, the Walsall players and the home fans. The relentless noise and the aggressive stance taken by the Millwall supporters continued throughout the game.

Not only were the fans full on, but so were the Millwall players. They tore into Walsall right from kick-off. Even Ricky Newman played a blinder! It was going to be our night and I was determined to enjoy it. Chances were being created with ease, and one eventually led to a goal by Richard Sadlier. The goal was scored at the opposite end to where the Millwall supporters were, but this failed to stop hundreds of Millwall fans steaming the pitch, many racing the length of the pitch to personally congratulate Sadlier for his efforts. There was no malice involved in this invasion, just pure joy. 1,900 people were watching their dream of a lifetime come true in front of their very eyes. Everyone has a dream in life, and many of these dreams will never, ever come true. For most football fans, the dream consists of their team achieving some sort of success. For most Millwall fans, the dream was to see the Lions walk out of the tunnel and onto the hallowed turf of Wembley. Sadlier's goal meant that this dream was turning into reality. Perhaps people with no interest in football may think our dreams are quite sad, and they may even be correct. But how many of these people can say they have actually seen their dreams come true? I would guess not many at all. Football really is a wonderful sport in so much as it brings so many people together and if ever you needed evidence of the importance of football to so many people, you only needed to witness the celebrations that followed this goal.

By half-time, a line of police had formed in front of the away end in a bid to prevent any further encroachment onto the playing surface. Even our chairman came to the front of the stand to plead with us to refrain from invading the pitch. Whilst I can fully understand his concerns at the possible consequences of our actions, I do not think he fully realised the extent of our joy. At this moment, I felt sorry for Theo. He knew there was no malice in the pitch invasion, but he also knew how the media would portray our actions to a gullible nation who hang on their every word. He was probably correct to try to calm us down, but this would never have worked in a month of Sundays.

The second half kicked-off in the same way the first half had ended. Millwall were running the game and the supporters continued the barrage of noise. Harris missed a few chances to extend our lead, and as the game drew to a close, Walsall slowly started having more possession. Inevitably, in the final minute, Walsall snatched an equaliser. As the ball hit the back of the net, the police officer in front of me muttered, "Oh shit!"

Millwall were still ahead on aggregate, but after coming so close to reaching Wembley, it would be just like Millwall to throw it away in the last minute. Had they done so, I think we would have been looking at serious trouble, a situation this particular policeman was only too aware of.

Millwall held out in injury time and as the final whistle blew, the police line failed to prevent a full scale pitch invasion from the delirious Lions fans. The players were just as excited as the fans and a full scale party erupted on the pitch. At the other end of the ground, a handful of Walsall fans made a half-hearted attempt to defend their pitch from the Londoners, but fortunately for them, the police spotted them before we did, and they were quickly sent home to think again. The party continued on the pitch as Errol Flynn yelled out "I believe in miracles!" over the tannoy, a very apt record to play under the circumstances.

I've been to plenty of football matches over the years, but this was one of the best nights I had ever had. To see so many people so happy was an incredible experience. These people may not all be angels, but a lot of us have to put up with a lot of bollocks because of who we are and who we support. To put up with such crap, for so many years, makes it difficult to follow your club in the way that all true supporters should. Despite the downsides to following the Lions, these 1,900 people had remained loyal throughout the hard times and were now being rewarded in the best possible way.

In the weeks after this game, my mind was on one thing and one thing only. I bored everyone with my relentless boasting about our impending Cup Final appearance against Northern giants, Wigan. Most of my friends who don't support Millwall had made it clear that they wished to come to the game with us. They knew that we would have a great day, whatever the final score, and wanted to enjoy the atmosphere and the all day drinking. I managed to get ten of the most expensive seats - after all it is not every season that Millwall play at Wembley so I thought I would treat myself. On top of this, my previous experiences of watching football at the venue of legends meant that I knew what a hovel Wembley really is. By purchasing a cheap seat, you were likely to be positioned behind a pillar with no chance of a clear view of the pitch.

As the big day approached, I became more and more excited. News was coming through that Millwall had sold 48,000 tickets for the game compared to a paltry 8,000 from Wigan. Wembley was going to be over run by Millwall supporters. I imagined the noise and passion emanating from the stands. The intimidation factor would surely play a crucial role in the outcome of the game. It would either inspire the Lions to produce a similar performance they produced at Walsall or it would work against us.

The Tuesday before the big day, we faced Colchester at the Den. Despite selling 48,000 tickets for Wembley, only 4,500 of us managed to turn up at the Den that night. I watched a reserve side cruise to a comfortable victory as I questioned what had happened to the other 44,000 loyal Lions fans.

CHAPTER 10

I awoke early on Sunday morning and continuously played the new Millwall CD that had been released to mark the occasion. Surprisingly, I had purchased some official merchandise from the club, and unlike most club songs, I actually thought these songs were above average.

I was in my local by 9:00am, the juke box was cranked up, and the beer was quickly flowing. We were in North London by opening time. We had decided to avoid the pubs at Baker Street and Wembley and elected to drink at Kensal Rise. This was only a short hop from Wembley on the tube, but would allow us enough time to get plenty of lager down our necks. After a few more beers we headed back to the tube station to make the final leg of our journey.

A couple of boys brought some food from the garage before jumping on the tube, so the rest of us waited outside the station for them to catch us up. Further up from the station was another pub, with a group of boys drinking outside. They had obviously spotted us and as we headed into the tube station, a few of them followed us. "Come on Wigan!" they shouted.

"We're fucking Millwall," we replied.

The boys apologised and returned to the pub. Who were these idiots? I had never seen any of them at Millwall before, but here they were giving it the big one, trying to play up to the tough reputation Millwall fans have. If any of these pricks had ever been to football they would have known we were Southerners by our appearance. Everyone who goes to football regularly knows you can easily spot the difference between a Northern firm and a Southern firm. The scene unfortunately was set for the rest of the day.

As we boarded the tube, I was amazed at the numbers of adults who had painted their faces blue and white. These were grown men acting like five year old children. I felt sorry for these people at first, but as they continued to declare their undying love for Millwall, they really started to annoy me. If they really loved Millwall, where had they been on Tuesday for the usual mundane fixture? Where had they been at Crewe on a Tuesday night, the previous season? How could this game mean as much to them as it meant to me? You don't suddenly become a loyal fan of a club by painting your face blue and mouthing off on a tube, but these idiots seemed to resent us being there because we hadn't joined in their party. Well, fuck these people, I know I will never have to rely on them when I risk my personal safety at places like Cardiff next season because they won't be there. They probably don't even know where Cardiff is.

As we walked along Wembley High Street, my mood got even worse. I have been to Wembley on quite a few occasions, but never had I seen so many police on duty. With all the idiots around, the police were left to concentrate on the ten of us as we walked to the ground, presumably as a result of us being dressed casually. We eventually managed to shake off our own personal escort as we approached the turnstiles. Here I saw a scene of thousands of painted faces frantically finishing off their cans of lager. I failed to spot any of the faces I normally see at Millwall.

Our big day had been hijacked by blue faced idiots behaving like complete pricks. I walked through puddles of piss and eventually found our row of ten seats and took my position, ready for the start of the game. Shortly before kick-off a group of blue faced idiots (with accompanying girlfriends) warned us we were in their seats. A quick check of their tickets revealed that their seats were in fact directly in front of us. One of my mates comes from Edinburgh, and despite leaving Scotland as soon as he could, he still has a Scottish accent. One of these idiots thought that as he had a strange accent, he must be a Wigan fan and started raring up at him. The bloke tried to look menacing in a bid to prove how hard he was in front of his gullible girlfriend, but really he just looked a complete twat. How can you have an argument or a fight with a grown man whose face is painted blue and whose hair was shaved to reveal "No-one likes us" on the back of his head? He soon shut up when he realised that my friend was not a lone Wigan fan amongst 48,000 Millwall fans. With his overwhelming odds of winning the fight suddenly reduced, he sat down and shut up.

A minute's silence was held to mark the tenth anniversary of the Hillsborough disaster, but the quiet was marred by a few idiots from both sides who failed to have the decency to keep quiet for just one minute. By now, I wanted to leave the ground and go and have a good drink away from all these retards. I stayed to watch the game, but got even angrier as I had to keep standing up in some bizarre ritual to prove to everyone how much I loved Millwall. Maybe these idiots who turned up for Wembley trips only felt that they had to demonstrate their love for Millwall by urging each other to stand up. My idea of proving your love for a particular club is to actually go to the games, but obviously this was not important to these fools.

The game itself was dire, with 0-0 written all over it. Despite the numbers, the noise generated by the Lions fans was very poor. Perhaps most of them did not know the words to *Let Them Come* and that is why they continually sang "Stand up if you love Millwall!", a song I had never heard once before in 13 years of watching the Lions home and away.

As the end of the 90 minutes approached, extra time loomed ominously ahead. I have to say I just wanted the game to end one way or another so I could get on with enjoying the day. Wigan scored deep into injury time, a crushing blow for Millwall as there was no time left to recover. That was it for me. I left my seat and left Wembley.

I was never really that bothered whether Millwall won or lost the game. The achievement was actually getting to Wembley to make the dream come true. When your dreams do come true and you realise that what you hoped for all your life turned out to be a waste of time, it does make you start to reassess your life. After we had beaten Walsall, I felt so happy for myself and all the other 2,000 or so loyal Millwall supporters for whom it meant so much. To see all these idiots jumping on the bandwagon was a terrible disappointment, but to be honest, I should have known it was always going to happen.

I have seen a similar situation with friends who have supported Chelsea and Arsenal throughout the lean years. Now that Chelsea and Arsenal have hit a purple patch, these fans have been frozen out by the clubs and replaced by fans who can't even pronounce the name of their latest foreign star. Fortunately for me, Millwall's purple patch only lasted a day, and the following week, the usual 6,000 hardcore loyal fans turned up at the Den to watch us play Preston.

I for one have lost the appetite for success as a result of witnessing 48,000 people jumping on a band wagon for one day. I had always dreamt of the day Millwall won the Premier League and England won the World Cup. The reality of this dream is that Millwall would be over run with glory hunters every week. I personally have more fun at away games such as Lincoln or York, where three or four hundred proper Millwall fans are present, than I would have if we played the likes of Man United or Arsenal every week in the Premier League. I used to love going to Eastern Europe to watch England play a meaningless friendly, and I would now rather do this than go to watch England in a World Cup Final and be surrounded by the Sheffield Wednesday choir, banging drums and whistling the theme tune to *The Great Escape*. Where were they in Poland in 1991 and Prague in 1992? Nowhere, because *The Sun* had not paid for them to go on a fully expensed trip, that's where.

Had England won the World Cup in 1990 or 1998, every man and his dog would have an opinion on football. It's bad enough now as it is, but if England were to win the World Cup, it would be even worse. Everyone who meets me soon become aware that I love Millwall and England, and they always seem to offer me their opinion on football and football violence. Most of them have never been to a game in their life and take their opinions from the likes of Garth Crooks and Andy Gray. I have to stand there and be polite, but it has now got to the stage where I can only talk about football if I know the other person actually goes to games.

Since the Wembley debacle, my ideals have changed. I no longer wish to see Millwall competing against Chelsea, Arsenal and the rest. In an ideal world, I would love to see Millwall return to the First Division, and then struggle every year to remain in that league. Instead of winning Cup finals, we would win relegation battles. I would have all the excitement of winning without actually achieving any recognised success. Finishing just above the relegation zone would be the equivalent of winning the league. My day trips would not revolve around Sky TV, yet I could still visit some fine stadiums, meet genuine fans from other clubs, and on some occasions, still witness real football rivalry in the pubs and streets outside these grounds. The Millwall support would remain much as it is now, genuine people with a real love for their club despite all the negative things that happen.

With regards to England, I would be happy for them to beat Scotland every year in a return to the traditional annual fixture. They should bring back the Home Internationals. After all, according to the people who promote football in this country, violence no longer exists. As the rise in violence was the sole reason for the demise of the Home Internationals, culminating in that balmy day in Glasgow in May, 1989, when 5,000 Englishmen took liberties in the mean streets of Glasgow, it stands to reason that if violence no longer exists in football, these fixtures should be reinstated. However, we all know that in reality the violence has never really gone away and that if England were to play in Cardiff, Glasgow or Belfast, the violence would be there for all to see. You need only recall the events in Dublin in 1995. The authorities should have the decency to admit that football related violence is still a real problem instead of pretending that it no longer exists in a bid to make football attractive to the new breed of fan.

I was looking forward to the end of the season. For the first time in my memory, I felt like I needed a break from Millwall, and football in particular. Hopefully, after a lazy summer, my passion would be rekindled. Our league form had gone down the pan following our exhausting Cup run. As often happens in these situations, each league game was meaningless and it was quite obvious from some of the players performances that they were also looking forward to the summer. My disillusionment led me to miss the final away game of the season at Reading, a game I had previously been looking forward to all season. Reading had moved to their new stadium, by all accounts the finest in our division, but I had decided that my visit could wait another season. As it turned out, the game was marred by a return to the unsociable behaviour so loved by some of the Millwall fans. A half-hearted attempt to invade the pitch and petty vandalism on the buses back into town gave the press further justification for their continued slander of all things Millwall.

Our old friends Man City had qualified for a play-off position and secured a trip to Wembley by disposing of Wigan. They were to face Gillingham, the pride of Kent, at the twin towers. Almost immediately, rumours started flying out of Moss Side that Millwall would be waiting for The Guvnors at Wembley. These mouthy idiots saw this as the ideal opportunity to seek some revenge on Millwall for the way we had made them a laughing stock earlier on in the season. This did make me chuckle - after all, we had played them twice already that season and both times their boys were conspicuous only by their absence. Now that 40,000 Mancs were in London to play Gillingham, they suddenly decided they were ready for Millwall. This just about summed up their mentality for me, but one thing it did prove was that rivalry between football fans will never be allowed to die, despite the best efforts of the money men. If a set of supporters are humiliated, in the way City were at Maine Road, they will never be able to live it down until they have achieved some sort of recognisable revenge. In my opinion, this is the main reason why football related violence will never be entirely eradicated from the game.

A prime example is the hatred many Millwall supporters feel for Everton. This stems from the 1974 clash when many Millwall supporters were stabbed in skirmishes inside and outside Goodison Park. Most Millwall fans now are too young to have been at that game, myself included, but many of us are brought up to never forget what happened that day and rest assured, whenever Millwall play Everton, there will be a very real possibility of serious disorder.

As we enter the new millennium, we all have to be aware of change. In most cases, change is for the better. However, the drastic changes that have taken pace in football over the last decade have not been viewed in a favourable way by a large minority of people who attend football. Perhaps we should put up with it and leave our outdated mentality in the twentieth century. However, going to football would become about as exciting as going to the supermarket if the money men have their way, and the outcome would be a victory for the new breed of fans who have taken over the game. I just hope and pray that the genuine fans, the people who really care about their clubs, the people who put up with verbal and physical abuse just so that they can watch their team, continue to hold out against the new breed. These are the *real* fans, and the new breed should never, ever be allowed to forget it.

POSTSCRIPT

In June 1999, the fixture list for the forthcoming 1999/2000 season was released. To all football fans, this is one of the most important days of the summer months, and despite my general apathy following the disappointing end to the 1998/99 season, I eagerly awaited news of our forthcoming games.

A friend phoned me on the morning the fixtures were released. "You've got Cardiff, away," he said.

"Don't wind me up," I replied. "The police would never let that happen."

For most of the previous season, Cardiff City looked like they would be promoted from Division Three, and a lot of Millwall boys had been keeping an eye on their progress. Everyone, and I mean everyone, knew what would happen when we played Cardiff. Despite confirmation that the fixture would indeed take place on the opening day of the season, I still suspected the police would have the common sense to change the date of the game, and when I found out that there was a music festival taking place in Cardiff that same weekend, I thought that would provide the South Wales police with the ideal excuse to postpone the game and then make it a lower profile mid-week game or a Sunday morning game. Incredibly, the game was allowed to go ahead.

The National Criminal Intelligence Service must also have been aware of the serious potential for violence at this game. All summer, messages had been posted on various websites from both Millwall and Cardiff fans, openly advertising the fact that both sets of fans were hell-bent on confronting each other. At the very least, the police should have been reading these messages and taking note. Is this not the point of the NCIS? To monitor the activities of the rival mobs?

On the day of the game, the Metropolitan Police failed to prevent hundreds of ticketless Millwall fans boarding an early morning train to Cardiff, despite the fact that the game was strictly all ticket. On arrival in Cardiff, the police let this mob of Millwall leave the station, despite knowing that hundreds of Cardiff fans were lying in wait. They had the powers to put them straight back on the train to London, powers that have been used countless times in the past by other police forces. To everyone's surprise, they chose to let the two mobs clash in a busy city centre on a Saturday morning.

Further problems could have occurred when Millwall supporters arriving in Cardiff for the game by coach were not even offered a police escort to the ground. Fortunately, the Cardiff boys have standards (unlike Birmingham) and ignored the coaches, preferring to save their welcome for the Millwall boys who travelled down on the train.

As I understand it, Millwall did quite well in Cardiff. There were hundreds of Cardiff fans waiting for Millwall and no doubt Cardiff will say they slapped Millwall all over the town. Fair play to them, they certainly had the quality and the quantity. Not many teams take a large mob into Cardiff though, and so Millwall may have earned a little more respect in football hooligan circles. However, Cardiff have to remember that there is the small matter of a return game at the Den. They should save their boasting until after that game.

The following day, the papers were full of horror stories. Apparently, the city centre was cordoned off and shoppers fled in panic as hundreds of Millwall fans went on the rampage. Apparently, it was organised on the internet, mobile phones were used, and the fans didn't even wear colours.

Of course, the blame was entirely down to the nasty Millwall fans who cause trouble at every game they attend. Funny how incidents on the same day at Reading, West Ham and Birmingham did not attract the same levels of condemnation. I read all the papers and couldn't believe how naive these journalists continue to be. Did they not consider for one moment the fact that hundreds of Cardiff fans were also intent on causing trouble? And why didn't they question the role played by the police? And why did nobody ask why plastic bottles were on sale in the ground when it was obvious they would be used as missiles?

The Welsh police and the safety officers must have known there would be hundreds of fans trying to fight each other all day. They **MUST** have known. Yet, the security measures taken were a farce. Thank God that Millwall Football Club and the Metropolitan Police take more care of away fans at the Den than their counterparts do in South Wales - otherwise there would be serious trouble at most home games.

A few simple steps should have been taken that day. The game should have been moved to a morning kick-off on the Sunday, the police should have escorted Millwall supporters to the ground, Cardiff City Football Club should not have sold items that could easily be used as weapons, and the police should have kept the Cardiff fans well away from the away end after the game. These steps may not have prevented all the trouble, but they certainly would have helped to reduce the potential for violence that surrounds high profile games such as this. All these measures are bleeding obvious to all football fans, yet the media continue to take the easy and fashionable option by laying the blame at the feet of Millwall Football Club and its supporters.

The media loves its folk devils. Skinheads, lager louts, single Mums, new age travellers, Millwall fans. Their stock in trade is stereotypes, very few of whom actually inhabit the real world beyond their ivory towers. They claim to be exposing football hooliganism, when all they are really doing is glorifying it in a bid to shift 'papers.

Millwall supporters are no angels, but that's just as well given the shit they have to take from the media, certain police forces, rival fans, and even their own club on occasions. The way football is going, I can't see things changing either. Not that I'll lose any sleep over it. As the song goes, no one likes us, and we don't care.

Also available

LET 'EM COME

- Millwall FC and supporters

Four track CD celebrating Millwall's first ever
Wembley appearance with the 1998-99 Cup final
squad backed by The Originator. Also includes
Roy Green's original version of *Let 'Em Come.*
£4.95 (post free) from:

STP Mail Order

P.O. Box 12, Lockerbie. DG11 3BW.
Please make cheques, postal orders payable to STP Mail Order.
We send books and CDs all over the world.

Bring out your riot gear

HEARTS
ARE HERE!

Welcome to an Edinburgh that doesn't exist in the tourist guides. An Edinburgh where youths fought each other over territory, style and football.

During the Eighties, Edinburgh's underbelly became a battlefield for mods, punks, skinheads and casuals. And as Hearts struggled on the pitch, it was their hooligan following that was making all the news. Towns and cities all over Scotland knew the meaning of Gorgie Aggro. It was the excitement of being part of an invading hooligan army that attracted C.S. Ferguson and his friends to Hearts, first as a young gang mod and then as one of the first recruits to the infamous Casual Soccer Firm.

Here's his story. Bring out your riot gear - Hearts are here!

Also includes an extract from Gavin Anderson's *Fighting For The Red, White And Blue.*

£8.99 (post free) from:
STP Mail Order
P.O. Box 12, Lockerbie. DG11 3BW.
Please make cheques, postal orders payable to STP Mail Order. We send books and CDs all over the world.

Football fiction

SATURDAY'S HEROES by Joe Mitchell
Price £3.95

It's all right for the mugs in their executive boxes and expensive seats to moan about football hooliganism. They've never had to defend their end against rival fans or fight their way back to a train station after an away game. But Paul West and his skinhead crew don't care what others think of them anyway. They live in a violent world that sees them do battle with casual gangs, other skinheads and rival supporters. A world that is slowly torn apart by aggro, a certain girl, and betrayal.

CASUAL by Gavin Anderson
Price £5.99

"The mob swayed towards the already rocking fence and buckling gates. The police constables looked on in horror as hundreds of hooligans crushed onto the side of the pens. A few of the coppers were already radioing for assistance, and when the higher ranking officers saw what was happening, they immediately ordered the gates to be unlocked. The ghost of Hillsborough still haunted them. The Chelsea firm burst through and shoved past the police and straight into the Red Army. A flare was fired from the Chelsea mob into the tightly packed opposition, instantly scattering them in all directions. The air was thick with bricks and bottles as running battles filled the street . . . "

Coming soon from

Terrace Banter

ST. GEORGE IN MY HEART
by John Mitchell
Price £8.99

John Mitchell takes you beyond the tabloid headlines to bring you this account of his days following England . . . "Wembley Way was packed full with fans, but not the type of supporters that Sky TV are now so fond on showing in their build up to games at the national stadium. Everyone here was part of a mob. There were 30 or so Derby fans, a mob of Boro fans, a particularly mean looking group of Bolton fans, and a huge mob of Birmingham fans. Obviously, all of the large London firms were present too. These mobs had been fighting each other every Saturday for years and years, but omn this particular night all of the old rivalries were to be temporarily laid to one side. Well, almost . . . "

SINGIN' THE BLUES
by Neil Nixon
Price £9.99

One man, one team, one love. Neil Nixon started supporting Carlisle United as a boy. Years later, he's still there. This is his story.

"Excellent, bloody excellent . . . By turns, hilarious, tragic and chillingly honest. This may well be the best book about one man and his team since Fever Pitch."
STEVEN WELLS, NME

for further details write to:
STP Mail Order
P.O. Box 12, Lockerbie. DG11 3BW.
**Please make cheques, postal orders payable to STP Mail Order.
We send books and CDs all over the world**

Come ahead if you think you're hard enough . . .

Terrace Banter was launched in October, 1998, as a football imprint of S.T. Publishing. Over the past decade football as a spectator sport has changed beyond all recognition, particularly for the ordinary fan. A great deal of working class culture and tradition is being cast to one side so that football can appeal to a new market, that of the "socca fan".

Through Terrace Banter we hope to put down in print the experiences of the ordinary fan before they are lost forever in a sea of plastic seats and replica strips. Unless we document our own history, it is left to outsiders and the mass media to be judge and jury.

This book is primarily about Millwall, but it is also about growing up on the terraces. We are interested in hearing from other authors who would like to publish a book about their exploits as a football supporter, no matter the team. Each book would represent a piece in a jigsaw puzzle, and together would give as good a picture of what life is like for the ordinary fan as you're likely to find.

Even if you don't think you could write the book yourself, we can help you get your words into print.

You can contact us at

Terrace Banter
S.T. Publishing
P.O. Box 12
Lockerbie
DG11 3BW
Scotland

stpbooks@aol.com